Plant Genetics

The Green World

Plant Genetics

Carl-Erik Tornqvist

Series Editor
William G. Hopkins
Professor Emeritus of Biology
University of Western Ontario

CHELSEA HOUSE
P U B L I S H E R S
An imprint of Infobase Publishing

Plant Genetics

Copyright © 2006 by Infobase Publishing

Chelsea House
An imprint of Infobase Publishing
132 West 31st Street
New York NY 10001

Library of Congress Cataloging-in-Publication Data

Tornqvist, Carl-Erik.
    Plant Genetics / Carl-Erik Tornqvist.
        p. cm. — (The green world)
ISBN 0-7910-8563-5
1. Plant genetics—Juvenile literature. I. Title. II. Green world (Philadelphia, Pa.)
QK981.T67 2006
581.3—dc22   2005032185

Chelsea House books are available at special discounts when purchased in bulk quantities for businesses, associations, institutions, or sales promotions. Please call our Special Sales Department in New York at (212) 967-8800 or (800) 322-8755.

You can find Chelsea House on the World Wide Web at http://www.chelseahouse.com

Text and cover design by Keith Trego

Printed in the United States of America

Bang 21C 10 9 8 7 6 5 4 3 2 1

This book is printed on acid-free paper.

All links, web addresses, and Internet search terms were checked and verified to be correct at the time of publication. Because of the dynamic nature of the web, some addresses and links may have changed since publication and may no longer be valid.

Table of Contents

Introduction

By William G. Hopkins

"Have you thanked a green plant today?" reads a popular bumper sticker. Indeed, we should thank green plants for providing the food we eat, fiber for the clothing we wear, wood for building our houses, and the oxygen we breathe. Without plants, humans and other animals simply could not exist. Psychologists tell us that plants also provide a sense of well-being and peace of mind, which is why we preserve forested parks in our cities, surround our homes with gardens, and install plants and flowers in our homes and workplaces. Gifts of flowers are the most popular way to acknowledge weddings, funerals, and other events of passage. Gardening is one of the fastest-growing hobbies in North America and the production of ornamental plants contributes billions of dollars annually to the economy.

Human history has been strongly influenced by plants. The rise of agriculture in the Fertile Crescent of Mesopotamia brought previously scattered hunter-gatherers together into villages. Ever since, the availability of land and water for cultivating plants has been a major factor in determining the location of human settlements. World exploration and discovery was driven by the search for herbs and spices. The cultivation of New World crops—sugar, cotton, and tobacco—was responsible for the introduction of slavery to America, the human and social consequences of which are still with us. The push westward by English colonists into the rich lands of the Ohio River Valley in the mid-1700s was driven by the need to increase corn production and was a factor in precipitating the French and Indian War. The Irish Potato Famine in 1847 set in motion a wave of migration, mostly to North America, that would reduce the population of Ireland by half over the next 50 years.

As a young university instructor directing biology tutorials in a classroom that looked out over a wooded area, I would ask each group of students to look out the window and tell me what they saw. More often than not, the question would be met with a blank, questioning look. Plants are so much a part of our environment and the fabric of our everyday lives that they rarely register in our conscious thought. Yet today, faced with disappearing rainforests, exploding population growth, urban sprawl, and concerns about climate change, the productive capacity of global agricultural and forestry ecosystems is put under increasing pressure. Understanding plants is even more essential as we attempt to build a sustainable environment for the future.

THE GREEN WORLD series opens doors to the world of plants. The series describes what plants are, what plants do, and where plants fit into the overall circle of life. *Plant Genetics* is a detailed look at the genetics of plants, through historical scientific achievements, discussions of genetic diversity, agricultural practices, and comparisons to animal and human genetics. Readers will learn about the origins of important crops and how plant breeders use genetics to improve crops. Details of some widely used methods in biotechnology are also included to demystify genetic engineering.

William G. Hopkins
Professor Emeritus of Biology
University of Western Ontario

1 History of Plant Genetics

*The land ethic simply enlarges the boundaries of the community
to include soils, waters, plants, and animals, or collectively: the land.*

— Aldo Leopold

History of Plant Genetics

GREGOR MENDEL

Gregor Mendel, known as the father of genetics, grew up in the early 1800s in Austria with a curiosity for math and science. At an early age, Mendel showed interest in the way things worked and how nature behaved. He worked on his family's farm until he was allowed to attend a special type of high school. Later, after finishing his secondary education, Mendel attended the University of Vienna. During his time in school, Mendel worked various jobs to pay for his tuition and living expenses. Eventually, Gregor Mendel became a monk in the monastery of St. Thomas in Brno, a city in what is now the Czech Republic.

Heredity and Garden Peas

During his time at the monastery, Mendel had a fascination with how different characteristics of plants were passed on from generation to generation—a process known as **heredity**. Heredity is the passing down of genetic information from parent to offspring and is the basis for the science of **genetics**. Mendel's favorite plant to work with was the garden pea. By carefully observing his garden, Mendel identified seven different characteristics, or **traits,** of the peas, each of which came in two forms. The seven traits Mendel observed were pod color, pod shape, seed color, seed shape, flower color, flower position on the stems, and plant height. On a given pea plant, the pod and seed color were either yellow or green. The flower color was either white or purple. The seed shape was either smooth or wrinkled. The pod shape was either full or pinched. The plant height was either tall or short. The flowers were found either at the tip of the branches or all along the branches. Mendel looked at all of these traits when describing the characteristics of the garden pea.

The seeds of Mendel's pea plant varieties gave rise to plants that had identical characteristics to the parents through each generation. The plants that produced this type of seed were called **true breeding** because the traits could be counted on to stay the same through each generation. The process of combining hereditary information from flower parents to form seeds is called fertilization. In fertilization, **pollen,** which carries the male reproductive cells, is transferred to the **stigma**, the female reproductive counterpart, in the flower and the creation of a seed is initiated (Figure 1.1).

In both plants and humans, the first cell to be formed as a result of fertilization is called a zygote. The first group of multiple cells is called an **embryo.** In humans, an embryo grows by adding cells, thereby becoming a fetus and then a baby. In plants, the embryo also accumulates cells but then becomes a dormant seed, which when germinated, starts to grow into a seedling. The earliest stage of fertilization in plants can be compared to the same process in humans. The human male reproductive cells, called sperm, come in contact with the female reproductive cell or **ovum** (egg), starting with zygote and then embryo development.

The resulting seeds from fertilization will grow into a plant that has **genetic material** from both of the parents. For the true breeding plants, the flowers are on the same plant, with either both male and female reproductive organs on one flower or on two separate flowers. Mendel's curiosity of the true breeding pea plants led him to hypothesize what would happen if he took pollen from one true breeding plant and applied it to the stigma of a flower on a true breeding plant with different traits than the male plant. The process Mendel used to combine the hereditary material of one plant with another plant is called **cross-fertilization** (or "crossing").

When pollen from a plant that was true breeding was crossed to another plant with different traits, Mendel found that certain crosses would always lead to **offspring** (i.e., the plants that grew from seeds made by the previous generation of pea plants) with characteristics that were both like and unlike those of either parent plant. These traits, he noticed, always appeared in the

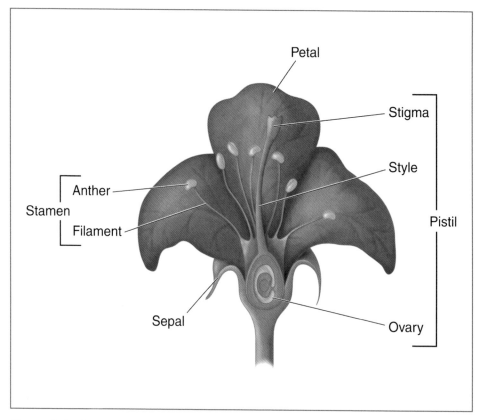

Figure 1.1 Fertilization is the process of combining hereditary information from flower parents to form seeds. In this process, pollen is transferred to the stigma in the flower and the creation of a seed is initiated.

same **ratio**, or relative numbers. Mendel wondered what would happen if he were to mix the different types of pea plants together. Because traits of offspring were believed to come about by mixing of genetic information from the two parents, Mendel wanted to test this hypothesis by seeing if pea plants resulting from crosses would show new traits, meaning traits not seen in either of the parent plants. If the **progeny,** or offspring, of this cross-fertilization had traits such as lavender-colored flowers, for example (mixing of white and purple), then Mendel could conclude that the parental traits were passed on equally and blended in the offspring. Instead, Mendel found the offspring had flowers that were always either white or purple, but never lavender. Thus the traits were not blended.

This observation led Mendel to conclude that the trait of a certain form, for example green seed color, was **dominant** to another form and would mask, or cover, the characteristic of the **recessive** form. The terms *dominant* and *recessive* refer to different forms, called **alleles**, of a trait. In Mendel's time, traits were believed to come from unknown hereditary material. We now know that this material is a **gene**. In humans, animals, and many plants, there are two alleles for each gene. Through many crosses, Mendel came to the conclusion that the seven traits could be traced to one gene each, made up of two alleles, which are either dominant or recessive. According to Mendel, if a plant has either one allele or two alleles of the dominant form of a gene, the plant shows the characteristic of the dominant allele and never of the recessive allele. However, if the plant has two alleles of the recessive type, then the plant shows the characteristic of the recessive allele for the given trait because no other form of the gene is present. The state of having both a dominant and a recessive allele of the same gene is called **heterozygous**. The state of having two of the same type of allele, either dominant or recessive, is called **homozygous**. By analyzing the characteristics of offspring and diagramming the crosses he made, Mendel was able to determine which seven of the 14 traits were dominant and which seven were recessive. Mendel concluded that tall plants, yellow seed color, green pod color, round seed coat, smooth pod, purple flower color, and flowers located all along the stem are the dominant forms of the respective trait.

Based on his observations, Mendel could make two generalizations about **inheritance**, or the passing down through generations, of traits. These generalizations have come to be known as Mendel's **laws of heredity**. The first law, called the law of segregation, states that traits are passed on through hereditary material for which each trait has two forms and, during formation of reproductive cells, each cell gets only one form of the hereditary material. The second law, called the law of independent assortment, states that alleles of genes **segregate**, or separate, independently of other genes' alleles when the parent plant makes reproductive cells (Figure 1.2).

Even though Mendel made many brilliant observations, the meaning of his work would not be known until 60 years later, in 1900. Carl Correns, Erich von Tschermak, and Hugo de Vries rediscovered Mendel's published articles on his pea plant experiments. These European scientists repeated Mendel's exact

Mendel's Experiments with Crosses

Mendel followed seven different traits in his garden peas from generation to generation. The genetic inventory of Mendel's garden varied to the point that pairs of plants had all seven to zero traits in common. In essence, Mendel could pick and choose plants with precise traits with which to perform crosses. Using this genetic resource to perform crosses, Gregor Mendel discovered his laws of dominance, segregation, and independent assortment.

The monohybrid crosses consisted of two parent plants with only one different trait—height. This allowed Mendel to discover the principles of dominance and segregation. The presence of one allele from a tall plant and one from a small plant in the offspring of a cross between true-breeding tall and small plants resulted in tall plants. Even though there was one small allele in all of the heterozygous offspring, the phenotype was always a tall plant. This observation led Mendel to his law of dominance: that some alleles of genes could mask, or cover, the presence of the other allele. When Mendel allowed the heterozygous peas to self-fertilize, the next generation was comprised of both tall and small plants, but there were three times more tall than small plants. This 3:1 phenotypic ratio is common in genetics.

experiments, performing the same crosses he had performed more than half a century earlier. The scientists found Mendel's results to be reproducible, and they published their own article in a scientific journal, giving credit to Mendel for his discoveries from decades before. The scientists brought attention to Mendel's work in a new scientific era, an era that would be accepting of his ideas about heredity.

BARBARA McCLINTOCK

Thirty years after the rediscovery of Mendel's laws and a century after Mendel carried out his experiments with peas, another

Self-fertilization of a plant that is heterozygous for a gene that singly controls a trait, with one allele dominant and one recessive, will always result in a segregating population of three-to-one dominant to recessive phenotype. This last result led Mendel to his law of segregation in which the two alleles of each gene in a heterozygote separate during production of reproductive cells.

Mendel's dihybrid crosses involved parent plants that differed in two traits. Mendel selected the traits for seed shape and color to follow the movement of the respective alleles during gamete formation. When pollen from a plant that produced wrinkled, green seeds was germinated on plants that produced round, yellow seeds, the next generation consisted of all plants having round, yellow seeds. When Mendel allowed these plants to self-fertilize, the result was a population with four different phenotypes segregating in a ratio of 9:3:3:1. The four seed phenotypes were round/yellow, round/green, wrinkled/yellow, and wrinkled/green. The new seed traits seen in the last generation proved to Mendel that alleles of genes move independently of each other during gamete formation because they made new combinations. This became Mendel's law of independent assortment.

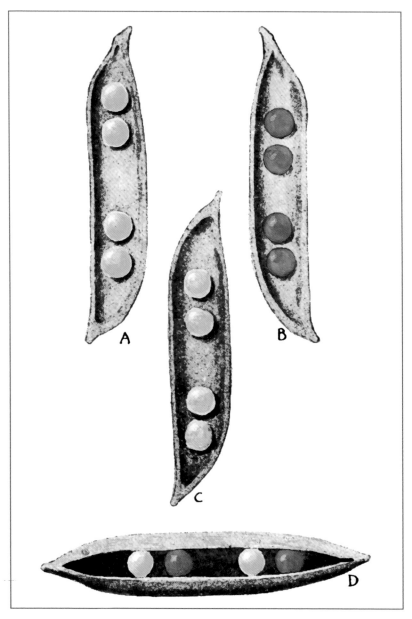

Figure 1.2 Mendel's experiments with peas evolved into Mendel's laws of heredity. Mendel crossbred peas that produced (A) yellow and (B) green peas. This produced a generation in which the peas were (C) yellow. By breeding the C generation peas together, Mendel discovered that the next generation had a mixture of (D) yellow and green peas.

young plant **geneticist** from the United States, named Barbara McClintock, was studying **chromosomes**, microscopic structures made of strands of genes from corn (known scientifically as *Zea mays*). McClintock was interested in studying the structure and behavior of the chromosomes in the **nuclei** of corn cells. Using corn as a model plant, McClintock was the first to discover **transposons**, which are genetic elements that can move about an organism's **genome**, a complete set of chromosomes containing all of the genes. Transposons are not found in every organism, but they are common in corn. If you have ever seen Indian corn, with the mosaic of colored kernels, then you have seen transposons at work (Figure 1.3).

Transposons and Corn

Transposons are small genetic elements that may contain an entire gene. Transposons get their name from their ability to undergo **transposition**, or movement, to new locations in the genome. Whether containing an entire gene or not, transposons have the ability to insert themselves in the genome in a random way. Therefore, a transposition event may result in a transposon inserting itself within a gene, thereby disrupting the gene's ability to reveal a trait. Some transposons can move on their own with an accompanying **enzyme**, or catalyst, called **transposase**. Others, called disabled transposons, require the presence and activity of an active transposon to be mobilized. Not all transposons are removed from the genome before moving to another location; **retrotransposons** are copied first and the copy is inserted in a new location, leaving the original copy in its place. So, there are two methods of transposing: the cut-and-paste method and the copy-and-paste method.

McClintock discovered a mechanism of mobilizing genes within a genome, but, since transposons didn't follow the Mendelian laws of inheritance, there were many skeptics of McClintock's work. Making McClintock's findings harder to

Figure 1.3 Transposons are genetic elements that can move about an organism's genome. Transposons are not found in every organism, but they are common in corn. This mosaic of colored kernels in Indian corn shows transposons at work.

impress upon the male-dominated scientific community was the discrimination against women that characterized the entire nation throughout most of the twentieth century. Although she received the highest award from the Genetics Society of America and served on the executive boards of many scientific organizations, McClintock's work was not taken seriously by the larger scientific community until decades later. Social barriers that kept women from reaching tenured positions at universities fueled the scientific community's rejection of McClintock's ideas.

It was not until later, when male scientists studying bacteria also found evidence of transposable elements, that McClintock's work on transposons in maize was given the attention it deserved. Since research on bacteria was deemed important, the fact that transposons could be found in this organism was extremely exciting to the general scientific community. McClintock soon received awards and became elected to several high posts in prestigious scientific societies. It was not until 1983, 50 years after her pioneering research on transposable elements in maize, that McClintock was given her highest honor: she was chosen as the recipient for the 1983 Nobel Prize in Physiology or Medicine.

OTHER MODELS OF GENETIC TRANSFER

There are other models of genetic transfer through generations that do not follow **Mendelian** principles. **Incomplete dominance** gives rise to alleles that are neither dominant nor recessive. Rather, the combination of the alleles that make a heterozygote leads to a physical appearance, or **phenotype**, showing the characteristics of both alleles. **Codominance** occurs when both alleles of a gene are dominant and the heterozygous **genotype** yields a phenotype that is a blending of the two traits (i.e., unlike that of either homozygous form). The carnation, for example, is a plant that expresses codominant alleles in flower color. Both the phenotypes of white and red flower color come from homozygous dominant genotypes. These can be designated WW for white and RR for red. The genotype of heterozygous dominant, or WR, leads to a pink flower. Because the genes for producing proteins that create white pigment are being expressed at the same level as the genes producing proteins for red color, the resulting flower looks pink—the color you get when you mix red and white. These genotypes and the associated phenotypes can be diagrammed using a **Punnett square**, named after Reginald Punnett, who was also an early geneticist (Figure 1.4).

In 2005, Dr. Susan J. Lolle at Purdue University published a research article in the journal *Nature* that described the inheritance of an allele in an ***Arabidopsis thaliana*** plant (a small plant in the mustard family) that had skipped the parent generation; in

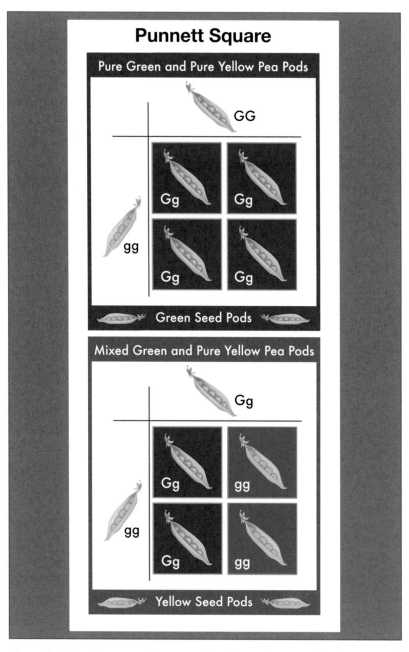

Figure 1.4 Genotypes and the associated phenotypes can be diagrammed using a Punnett square. This Punnett square shows the possible combinations of offspring that can be found from pure and mixed pea pods.

other words, the allele was from the grandparent plant. The fact that the genetic makeup of the current generation of the *Arabidopsis* plant in Dr. Lolle's hands had alleles that could not have been inherited from either parent, according to Mendel's principles, was mysterious. Dr. Lolle and her colleagues are currently working to decipher this genetic puzzle. Mendel's genetic principles have stood the test of time, but with advanced scientific research, more exceptions to his rules are being discovered.

Gregor Mendel and Barbara McClintock are alike in that the impacts of both scientists on the scientific community were not recognized until long after they did their research. Mendel was far ahead of his time, and his observations have been fundamental to our understanding of genetics today. McClintock's pioneering work on maize chromosomes and transposition has been invaluable to the field of **cytogenetics.**

Mendel's observations on the genetics of peas explained how alleles of genes can recombine in different combinations upon fertilization. The assortment of the alleles among the resulting **gametes,** or sex cells, is random, but the location of the alleles is always at the same position on the chromosome. Using corn chromosomes, McClintock studied a mechanism in which genetic elements move about the genome in a random fashion, leading to new chromosomal compositions with genes in completely different locations than those found in the parent or previous **generations.**

2 Overview of Genetics

A modern gene codes for something.
— John M. Smith

Overview of Genetics

DNA: THE BUILDING BLOCKS OF LIFE

The basic building blocks of life that hold the genetic information are **nucleic acids**, which are chemicals found in the cells of all organisms, from bacteria to sunflowers to humans. Nucleic acids can be described as having three distinct chemical parts: (1) a phosphate group, which is a phosphate atom surrounded by four oxygen atoms; (2) a type of sugar, known as pentose; and (3) a ring-like molecule, called a base. Two different types of ring structures characterize the bases: a single five-sided ring (a pentagon shape) and a double ring consisting of a five- and a six-sided ring joined at one side (Figure 2.1). The single-ring base is called a **pyrimidine**, and the double-ring base is called a **purine**.

There are two types of nucleic acid molecules crucial for life; these are **deoxyribonucleic acid (DNA)** and **ribonucleic acid (RNA)**. The prefixes *deoxyribo-* and *ribo-* describe the type of sugar molecule attached to the acid. The *deoxy-* in DNA means that the sugar in this nucleic acid is missing an oxygen atom (*de-* means "without"); the sugar in RNA has that oxygen atom (Figure 2.2). This simple difference in the chemical composition of DNA and RNA is important to the structures and characteristics of these molecules.

DNA and RNA each come in four different types, called **nucleotides,** based on how additional atoms are attached at different points on the base-ring structure. For DNA, the names of the four nucleotides are adenine, thymine, cytosine, and guanine. Adenine and guanine are purines, while cytosine and thymine are pyrimidines. RNA also has four nucleotides; all but one are the same as in DNA. Instead of thymine, the fourth RNA nucleotide is uracil, which is also a pyrimidine. The difference between thymine and uracil is the presence of an extra chemical component called a methyl group, attached to the uracil ring. In order for multiple nucleotide molecules to fuse together to make a DNA or RNA chain, the phosphate group from each nucleotide bonds to the sugar component of the neighboring nucleotide. When all of

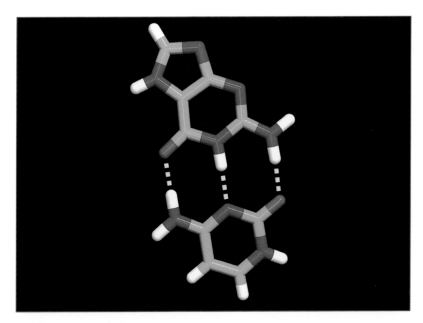

Figure 2.1 Two different types of ring structures characterize the bases: a single five-sided ring (pyramidine) and a double ring consisting of a five- and a six-sided ring joined at one side. This cytosine-guanine base pair are the nucleic acids that bond in a DNA chain. The atoms are carbon (green), nitrogen (blue), hydrogen (white), and oxygen (red). Cytosine is a pyrimidine (bottom), and guanine is a purine (top).

the nucleotides are connected in a chain, the nucleic-acid molecule forms a sugar-phosphate backbone (Figure 2.3). The properties of DNA and RNA are not identical, but they share common nucleotides. Because the nucleotides of DNA and RNA are similar, we will focus the rest of the discussion in terms of DNA.

DNA Double Helix

In the cell, DNA is in the form of a double helix, which is like a ladder that has been twisted lengthwise (Figure 2.4). Each side of the ladder is a chain of connected nucleotides. The helix is double because the nucleotides are found in pairs. The bases of a pair are always the same: cytosine pairs with guanine and adenine pairs with thymine. The bases that pair with each other are called

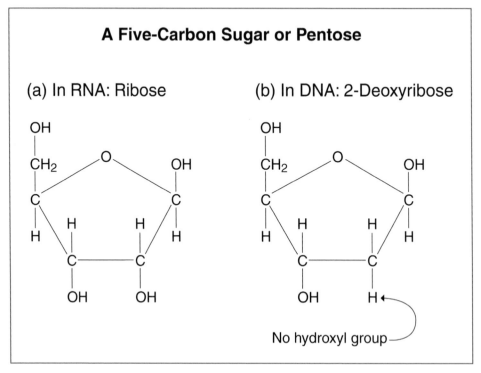

A Five-Carbon Sugar or Pentose

(a) In RNA: Ribose

(b) In DNA: 2-Deoxyribose

No hydroxyl group

Figure 2.2 The structural component of a nucleic acid includes a type of sugar called a pentose. A pentose has a single five-sided ring structure. An RNA ribose molecule includes a hydroxyl group (OH on each side of the bottom sides), whereas a DNA 2-deoxyribose molecule does not. The *deoxy-* in DNA means that the sugar in this nucleic acid is missing an oxygen atom; the sugar in RNA has that oxygen atom.

complementary bases, which form the rungs of the ladder. The nucleotides that make up the sides of the ladder are called complementary strands. Because each nucleotide has only one complementary partner, one can figure out the order, or **sequence**, of the second strand if only the sequence of the first strand is known. When geneticists talk of DNA sequence, they are referring to the order of the nucleotides on the strand. The association of the nucleotide pairs is based on hydrogen bonds. Although hydrogen bonds are not as strong as the phosphate-sugar bonds of the DNA backbone, this base pairing makes the double helix of DNA a very strong structure.

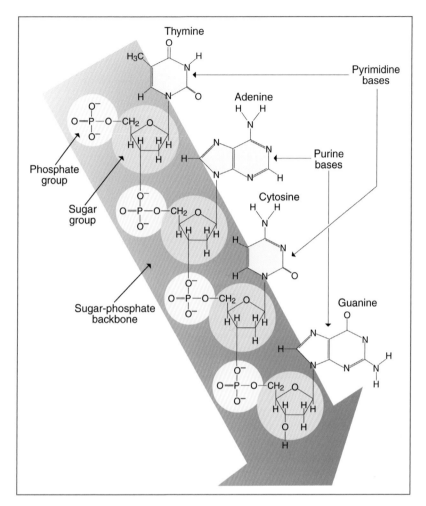

Figure 2.3 Multiple nucleotide molecules fuse to make a DNA or RNA chain by bonding the phosphate group from each nucleotide to the sugar component of the neighboring nucleotide. When all of the nucleotides are connected in a chain, the nucleic acid molecule forms a sugar-phosphate backbone.

Blueprint for Proteins

The nucleotide bases of DNA can be written in shorthand as A, C, G, and T, for adenine, cytosine, guanine, and thymine, respectively. Geneticists use this notation to write a DNA sequence. Protein products are made according to the DNA sequence,

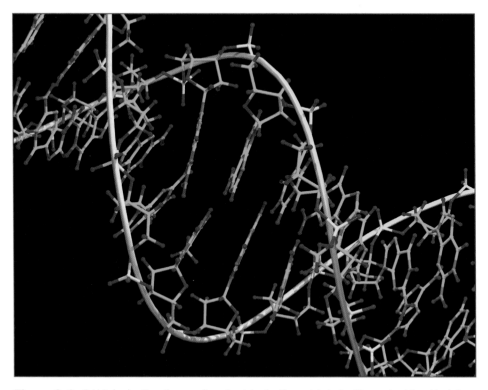

Figure 2.4 DNA is in the form of a double helix, which is like a ladder that has been twisted lengthwise. Each rung of the ladder is a chain of connected nucleotides. The helix is double because the nucleotides are found in pairs. The bases of a pair are always the same: cytosine pairs with guanine and adenine pairs with thymine. The nucleotides that make up the sides of the ladder are called complementary strands–nucleotide bases (blue-red) project from the outer phosphate backbone (yellow).

which is **transcribed** to messenger RNA (mRNA) and then, by way of transfer RNA (tRNA), **translated** into **amino acids**, which are the building blocks of proteins. There are only 20 amino acids in nature that combine to make proteins found in all organisms.

The series of amino acids needed to make a particular protein is determined by **codons**, the triplet language of RNA. One can think of codons as "words" that are three letters long; the letters of the nucleic acid "alphabet" being A, C, G, and T (or U for uracil in RNA). Since amino acids are translated from RNA, the codon alphabet that represents them is made up of the letters A, C, G, and U. Some amino acids have only one codon that represents them, while others may be represented by up to six different codons. In addition to amino acids, there are three codons, called stop codons, that signal the end of translation and one codon that signifies the start of translation (AUG, which codes for the amino acid methionine). Stop codons do not code for an amino acid; they simply signal the translational machinery to stop.

Chromosomes

Mendel thought of genes as pieces of material with information about how to create certain traits. These genetic elements could be inherited by offspring, and the traits would appear in certain ratios that Mendel could predict by knowing the genetic makeup of the parent plants. It was not until after Mendel's time that the word *gene* would be used to describe the genetic elements, or alleles, that Mendel had been studying. Geneticists during Mendel's period could observe the results of crosses and could determine phenotypes of plants, but that was as far as they could go. During McClintock's days as a young researcher, great strides were taking place in the field of genetics. Scientists discovered that the genetic elements Mendel described were genes located on thread-like structures, called chromosomes, in the nucleus of a cell.

The nucleus, a membrane-bound structure within a cell, contains all of a cell's genetic material, or genome. Chromosomes are found in twisted bundles that are held together by **nuclear** proteins called **nucleosomes**. Nucleosomes can be thought of as having a barrel shape, around which DNA is wound, like string around a spool. Together, the chromosome strands and the nucleosomes make **chromatin**, the fundamental structure of chromosomes (Figure 2.5). It is from these thread-like bundles that all of the genes, in the form of DNA, are transcribed into mRNA, which, in turn, is translated into amino acids that join together to form proteins.

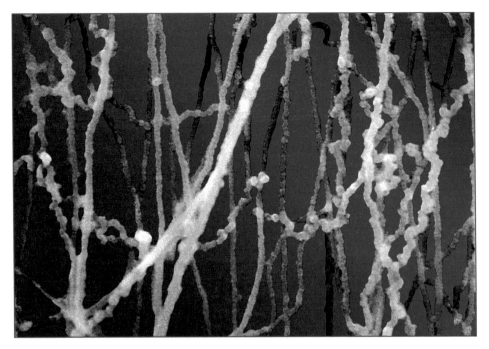

Figure 2.5 Chromosome strands and nucleosomes make chromatin, the fundamental structure of chromosomes. Through these thread-like bundles, all genes in the form of DNA are transcribed into mRNA, which is then translated into amino acids that join to form proteins.

Transcription and Gene Expression

Genes are transcribed with the help of DNA-specific and RNA-specific enzymes and then are translated into amino acids by specialized enzymes that form complexes, referred to as **ribosomal** complexes. When the transcriptional enzymes encounter a gene to be expressed, the usual binding point of the enzyme complex on the chromosome is at a site before the actual start of the gene. The area before the gene is called the **promoter,** which is a stretch of sequence that is recognized by the transcriptional machinery of the cell as the site onto which the RNA polymerase enzyme should attach. There may be additional sequences before or after the gene or within **introns** (the noncoding regions of the gene) that regulate the expression of the associated gene. These additional

DNA sequences are called **enhancers** or **silencers**, depending on whether gene expression is increased or decreased. The regulatory region has a unique sequence that is recognized by transcription factors. Most transcription factors have two domains, or sections, that affect the expression of the target gene. A DNA-binding domain allows the transcription factor to bind to the actual DNA of the enhancer or silencer. The other domain is a transcriptional activator that associates with RNA polymerase enzymes to either activate or suppress transcription of the gene. Once the enhancer or silencer region of a gene is recognized, the appropriate action will occur: either more or less **expression** of the gene.

Spotlight on Cytogenetics

The study of cells is called cytology and the study of genes is called genetics. Hence, the study of genes at the cellular level, or scale, is called cytogenetics. Since chromosomes are large clusters of **DNA** strands that encode genes, the focus of cytogenetics is chromosome structure and number. Cytogeneticists use many special skills and tools to study the character of chromosomes. The techniques used by cytogeneticists who research plants are the same as those who study animals. Regardless of the organism, a technique called chromosome painting is used to identify the different chromosomes in a set. Chromosome painting uses special chemical dyes to "paint" a pattern on a chromosome. Different dyes "stick" to different parts of a chromosome, creating a unique pattern for each chromosome in the set. A cytogeneticist studies the condition of a chromosome by viewing it under a microscope. Chromosome maps are used to identify the placement of genes along chromosomes. An ordered display of all of the chromosomes in a cell is called a karyotype. Cytogeneticists may karyotype the amniotic fluid of a pregnant woman to make sure that the baby will be healthy. A plant may be karyotyped to investigate its lineage or ancestral origins.

3 Meiosis, Mitosis, and Alternation of Generations

The flower is the poetry of reproduction.
It is an example of the eternal seductiveness of life.

— Jean Giraudoux

Meiosis, Mitosis, and Alternation of Generations

MEIOSIS

The basis of Mendel's law of independent assortment can be understood by examining the cellular process of **meiosis**. Meiosis is the double cell division event that results in four **daughter cells,** each with half of the genetic content of the original **mother cell.** The cells of the male and female **gametophytes**—the pollen grain and **embryo sac**—result from the cell divisions of meiosis. Cell division by way of meiosis is best described by breaking down the two divisions into their four stages or phases (Figure 3.1). The Roman numeral after each phase represents the division of meiosis.

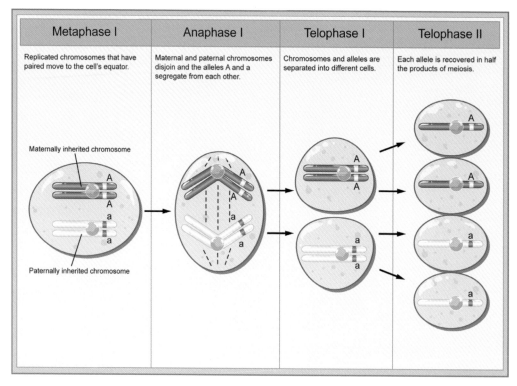

Metaphase I	Anaphase I	Telophase I	Telophase II
Replicated chromosomes that have paired move to the cell's equator.	Maternal and paternal chromosomes disjoin and the alleles A and a segregate from each other.	Chromosomes and alleles are separated into different cells.	Each allele is recovered in half the products of meiosis.

Maternally inherited chromosome

Paternally inherited chromosome

Figure 3.1 Meiosis is the basis of Mendel's law of independent assortment. Meiosis is the double cell division event that results in four daughter cells, each with half of the genetic content of the original mother cell. Meiosis divides cells through phases—prophase (not pictured), metaphase, anaphase, and telophase.

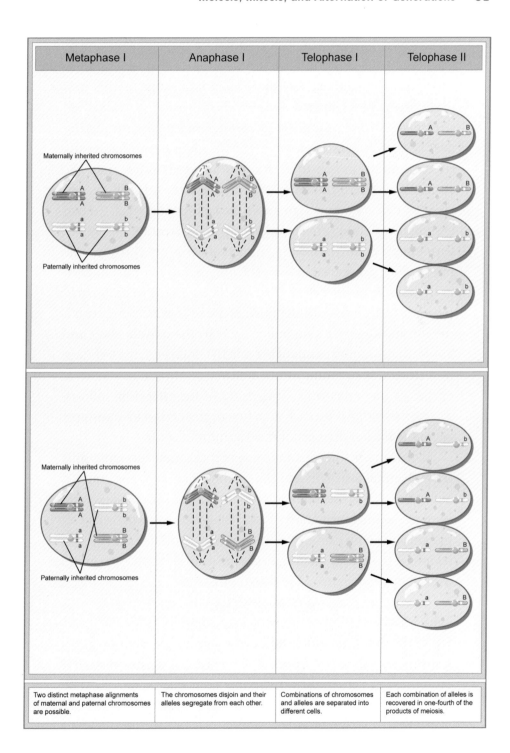

Metaphase I	Anaphase I	Telophase I	Telophase II
Two distinct metaphase alignments of maternal and paternal chromosomes are possible.	The chromosomes disjoin and their alleles segregate from each other.	Combinations of chromosomes and alleles are separated into different cells.	Each combination of alleles is recovered in one-fourth of the products of meiosis.

The initial state of the cell is prophase I: the chromosomes have doubled but are not yet distinguishable from each other. Then, in late prophase, the duplicated sister chromatids pair up and can be identified because the chromatid strands are stretched. At this point, the phenomenon known as crossing over occurs. A crossover event occurs when homologous sister chromatids attach to each other at points other than the **centromere**. Where the sister chromatids join, a break occurs, allowing chromosomal segments to be swapped between the two chromatids. Crossing over is a key step in the creation of gametes with unique genotypes. Next, in metaphase I, the chromosome pairs, which are joined at the centromere, are centrally aligned in the middle of the cell, and **spindle fibers** attach to each chromosome of each pair. In the third phase of meiosis, anaphase I, the chromosome pairs are pulled apart by the spindle fibers and are drawn to opposite ends of the cell. In telophase I, the last stage in meiosis I, the chromosomes are completely at opposite ends of the cell and **cytokinesis**, or division of the **cytoplasm**, follows. The two resulting cells, each with two copies of the chromosome, begin the second division of meiosis, or meiosis II.

In meiosis II, the chromosomes go through the same four stages as in meiosis I, except the chromosomes are not doubled in prophase II, as they were in prophase I. This difference is what leads to the final formation of four daughter cells with only half the chromosome number as the original mother cell. Also, in telophase II, nuclear membranes form around the chromosomes in each new daughter cell prior to cytokinesis.

Cytokinesis

Up to the point of cytokinesis, every step in cell division is the same in animals as it is in plants. The division of the cell's cytoplasm, called cytokinesis, differs between plants and animals. This difference is most likely due to the presence of both a cell wall and a plasma membrane around plant cells, and not just a plasma membrane, as is the case in animal cells. In human cells, division occurs by a pinching method that gradually narrows the cytoplasmic space between the two opposite sides on the division plane. Eventually, the plasma membranes from either side of the cell meet in the middle and fuse together, creating two separate cells. In plant cells, the division process is very different. Following telophase, when the chromosomes are at either end of the mother cell, a new cell wall begins to grow along the division plane from opposite sides of the cell; ultimately, this cell wall comes together to produce a solid wall separating the two daughter cells. When the chromosome pairs are pulled apart, after crossing over, different pieces of the chromosome pairs can stay attached to each other, resulting in a break in the chromosome strand and in more chromosome material on one side and less on the other. This means that some of the daughter cells would be deficient in the genes that were on the lost chromosome pieces. This event would result in the newly arising cells having abnormal genetic content, as proposed by McClintock. Mendel saw, without the aid of a microscope, that the process of creating gametes somehow resulted in new traits found in the progeny pea plants. It is the resulting cells, or gametes, of meiosis that merge from both parent plants to form the **zygote**, the first cell of the offspring plants.

MITOSIS
Sexual Reproduction and Gamete Formation
The first cell of the progeny is actually a fusion of a **haploid** nucleus from the female and from the male plant. Therefore, the new zygote that will form into an embryo and, in most plants, eventually a seed has a mixture of the two parents' genetic makeup. The special cells for reproduction, or gametes, contain only half of the chromosome number (haploid) as the rest of the plant. These cells reside in a specialized part of the plant called the **sporangium**, within

Theory of the Breakage-Fusion-Bridge Cycle

Barbara McClintock's first major pioneering theory was the breakage-fusion-bridge cycle. By describing the chromosome structure, the concept of the breakage-fusion-bridge cycle was McClintock's way of explaining the presence or absence of genes in the offspring of corn whose reproductive cells had been mutated by X-rays. X-ray mutations caused whole chromosome segments to be chopped off and reattached in different ways. Often, broken chromosomes would attach to homologous partners at the breakage site. This led to chromosomes that were dicentric, or had two centromeres. McClintock proposed that, due to their structure and to crossover events, dicentric chromosomes could be torn apart during meiosis and become rearranged in other ways in the resulting gametes (See Figure).

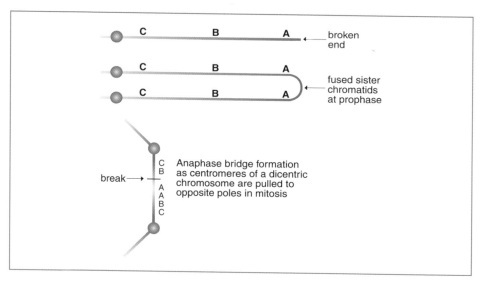

Figure: The broken end of the chromosome is caused by X-ray bombardment and is where the two homologous partners fuse. When spindle fibers attach to the two centromeres and pull to opposite poles of the cell, an anaphase bridge is formed that eventually breaks under the tension created by the contracting spindle fibers. The broken sister chromatids are each pulled to opposite poles where they become part of the chromosome set of the new daughter cells. The broken ends fuse to homologous chromosomes in the daughter cell in subsequent cell divisions and the cycle continues.

which the haploid cells are produced. These haploid cells, which have only one complete set of chromosomes in the nucleus, are generated by two consecutive meiotic events and one round of **mitosis**. Mitosis is another type of cell division, but instead of ending up with half of the chromosome number, as in meiosis, the daughter cells have exactly the same number of chromosomes as the mother cell. Mitosis is involved in division of cells that are not reproductive, like in the shoots, roots, and leaves (Figure 3.2).

In male flowers or in male parts of bisexual flowers, the **microsporocyte** is the **diploid** cell that, through meiosis, gives rise to four microspores. The four cells complete mitosis to form two pollen grains each, resulting in a total of eight pollen grains for each microsporocyte. Each pollen grain consists of two cells: one called the generative cell and the other called the tube cell.

In the female flower or flower parts, the diploid cell responsible for gamete production is called the **megasporocyte**. The megasporocyte goes through meiosis I and II, resulting in four haploid cells called **megaspores.** Only one of the four resulting cells survives to undergo three mitotic divisions. The resulting female gametophyte, created by three cell divisions of one megaspore, is multicellular.

Upon pollination of a female flower, the generative cell divides to become two sperm cells. When a pollen grain lands on a female flower, the tube cell will elongate and grow down into the ovary, where the mature, female gametophyte can be reached. In a process called **double fertilization**, each sperm cell releases its nucleus into the embryo sac; one sperm fertilizes the egg cell that will become the diploid zygote, while the other fertilizes the two nuclei of the large central cell to form **triploid** (3n) endosperm tissue (Figure 3.3). The endosperm tissue serves as the nutrient source for the plant embryo during seed germination. The yellow part of a corn kernel is the endosperm, which, in this case, makes up the majority of the seed.

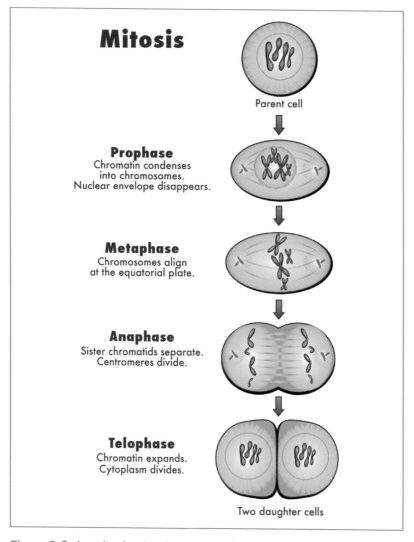

Mitosis

Parent cell

Prophase
Chromatin condenses into chromosomes. Nuclear envelope disappears.

Metaphase
Chromosomes align at the equatorial plate.

Anaphase
Sister chromatids separate. Centromeres divide.

Telophase
Chromatin expands. Cytoplasm divides.

Two daughter cells

Figure 3.2 In mitosis, the daughter cells have exactly the same number of chromosomes as the mother cell. Mitosis is involved in division of cells that are not reproductive, like in the shoots, roots, and leaves. Like meiosis, mitosis has four phases—prophase, metaphase, anaphase, and telophase.

ALTERNATION OF GENERATIONS

In flowering plants, the gametophyte is in the flower, which produces the seed; the rest of the plant, which is called the

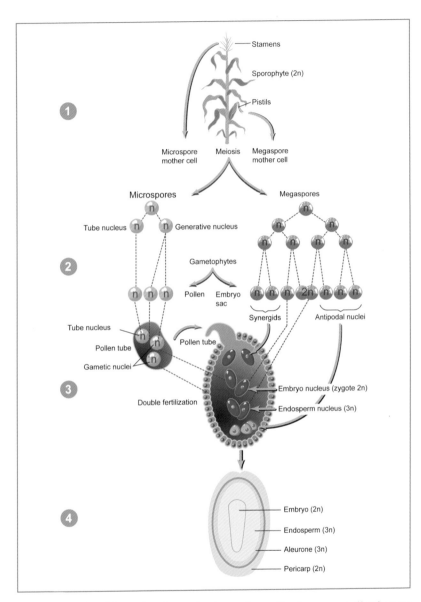

Figure 3.3 The life cycle of corn is shown here. Each sperm cell releases its nucleus into the embryo sac; one sperm fertilizes the egg cell that will become the diploid zygote, while the other fertilizes two nuclei of the large central cell to form triploid (3n) endosperm tissue. The endosperm tissue serves as the nutrient source for the plant embryo during seed germination. The yellow part of a corn kernel is the endosperm, which makes up the majority of the seed.

sporophyte, has a diploid chromosome number. However, in nonvascular plants such as mosses, the haploid part of the plant is most of what we see. This transition from haploid to diploid and again to haploid state is unique to plants and is called **alternation of generations.** Alternation of generation means that all plants have both a gametophytic phase and a sporophytic phase as part of their life cycle. In flowering plants, the sporophytic phase can be thought of as the **vegetative** state, or the state in which the plant grows branches and produces a lot of leaves. The gametophytic generation of vascular plants is confined to the small inconspicuous organs dedicated to the purpose of reproduction. In nonvascular plants such as mosses, liverworts, and hornworts, the gametophytic generation is the green part that we see; the sporophytic generation is much smaller and less visible (Figure 3.4).

Other Modes of Reproduction

Plants do not have to undergo fertilization in order to reproduce. They can also reproduce, or **propagate, asexually** (i.e., without fertilization), which is a characteristic known as vegetative reproduction. All plant cells have the ability to become any specialized cell of the plant. This characteristic of plant cells to become any type of cell is called **totipotency.** The act of becoming a specialized cell is called **differentiation,** and plant cells become differentiated just after forming in the cell-producing area called the **meristem.**

The undifferentiated cells found in the meristem are a type of **stem cell**, like the stem cells of humans. Recent media coverage has brought attention to research conducted on two different forms of human stem cells: those found in embryos and those found in the **bone marrow,** or the center of the bone, of adults. The meristematic cells of plants are more like the human stem cells found in embryos because, like this type of human stem cell, plant stem cells can become any type of specialized cell and, thus, any type of organ. Adult stem cells found in bone marrow, on

Figure 3.4 Alternation of generation means that all plants have both a gametophytic phase and a sporophytic phase as part of their life cycle. This carpet moss has distinct sporophytes growing on gametophytes (the visible green part). Sporophytes reproduce asexually whereas gametophytes reproduce sexually.

the other hand, can only be conditioned to become certain types of cells. Unlike human cells, a plant cell can **dedifferentiate** and become a cell that is completely different than the type of cell it was before. Dedifferentiation is the process in which a plant cell loses all of its specialized structures and **organelles**, which are the membrane-bound structures within the cell, and becomes a simple cell containing only the nucleus and the essential organelles needed for survival. Scientists can manipulate a dedifferentiated cell to become a particular cell by exposing it to various **hormones** that induce gene expression changes and affect development of the cell. The genetic basis of these **physiological** processes will be discussed further in chapter 6.

One touch of nature makes the whole world kin.

— William Shakespeare

Polyploid Plants

POLYPLOID PLANTS ARE ALL AROUND US

Have you ever bitten into a seedless watermelon and wondered why there were no seeds in the fruit? The reason is that the seeds are just never made. In fact, seedless watermelons are the result of plant breeding that involves the cross-fertilization of different **cultivars**, or subspecies, of plants.

Remember that cross-fertilization is the act of taking pollen (i.e., the male sex cell) from the flower of one plant and putting it on the stigma (i.e., the female reproductive organ) of another plant. The DNA from the pollen "fuses" with the DNA in the female plant to form the first cell, called a zygote. The zygote divides into many cells and makes a seed. In seedless watermelons, however, the seeds never form. Normally, pollinating a flower triggers both fruit and seed development. Seedless watermelons grow fruit but not seeds (with the exception of a few "false seeds"). The small, white "seeds" you may find in a seedless watermelon cannot grow to be plants and are called false seeds.

Seedless watermelons do not develop seeds because of the DNA in the nucleus of the zygote. Remember, the genetic material in this first cell comes from both the male and female plants. If the amount of DNA from each parent is different, then fertilization results in a cell with an amount of genetic content unlike that of either parent. The DNA that the seedless watermelon has in its reproductive cells is not distributed evenly. Therefore, the reproductive cells of the seedless watermelon have too much or too little genetic information. Without the "right" genetic information, meaning the type and amount of genes, the watermelon cannot create a normal seed. When the seedless watermelon is cross-fertilized with pollen from a seed watermelon, the resulting fusion of DNA is not balanced and cannot make a seed. The male watermelon plant has balanced DNA content in its gametes (sex cells), so it can reproduce normally on its own. The female plant, however, has uneven pairing of chromosomes (DNA strands) when it makes the reproductive cells in the process of meiosis, so it cannot reproduce on its own.

The genetic content of the fruit is separate from the seed because the fruit comes from only the mother cells. The female structure on the plant that becomes the fruit is the ovary of the flower. Thus, stemming from floral organs of the mother plant, the fleshy part of the melon contains DNA only from the plant on which it grows.

The cells that are in the fleshy part of the watermelon are not created by the reproductive process. Cells of this type, like in humans, are called **somatic**, or body, cells. Chromosomes are usually paired to matching partners in somatic cells. If there is only one pair of each type of chromosome in the nucleus of each somatic cell, then an organism is said to be diploid (*di* meaning "two," and *ploid* meaning "chromosome set"). The condition of having multiple sets of chromosomes in the gamete is called **polyploidy** (*poly* meaning "many"). The seedless watermelon is a triploid, meaning it has three sets of chromosomes in its somatic cells. The triploid is formed by the hybridization of a diploid with a **tetraploid** (*tetra* meaning "four"). The gamete of the diploid has one chromosome set (haploid), and the tetraploid gamete has two (diploid). With cross-fertilization, the number of chromosome sets in the haploid is added to the number in the diploid gamete, giving a total of three chromosome sets in the zygote. This zygote becomes the seed that grows into the seedless watermelon mother plant.

One might ask how a tetraploid watermelon would exist in nature, and the answer would be that it does not. The tetraploid watermelon is actually created by plant breeders who treat normal diploid watermelon plants with a chemical that makes the chromosome number double. The chemical, called **colchicine**, comes from the autumn crocus plant. Colchicine works by preventing cell division during mitosis. In mitosis, the chromosomes line up in the center of the cell where they are copied to make pairs. When introduced into the cell during mitosis, colchicine disables the fibers that pull the chromosome pairs apart prior to cell division. Since the chromosomes do not move from the cell center, the cell cannot divide and, therefore, retains the doubled-chromosome content.

Polyploidy

In earlier chapters, plants and humans were described as having very similar genetic material and machinery, but the genetics of plants and humans also differ. One major difference is in the ability of many plant species to thrive when they are polyploid. While not all plants exhibit this characteristic, more than half of all known flowering plants are polyploid. The cells in all organisms—from garden peas and corn to mice and humans, etc.—have a specific amount of DNA in their nuclei that gives the right dose of the necessary genes for healthy development. In polyploid plants, the DNA content in the nuclei of cells is multiplied because there is at least one additional set of chromosomes. The extra DNA, in many cases, means bigger than normal cells.

In humans, however, polyploidy is detrimental. Humans can only have two sets of chromosomes, making them diploid. The reason humans cannot be polyploid is because of the sex chromosomes. Sex chromosomes contain many important genes that need to be balanced with each other. Out of the numerous families that make up the plant kingdom, there are only a few plants, like the willow, that have sex chromosomes. In a polyploid, when chromosomes are pulled apart during meiosis, the unpaired or extra chromosomes will move randomly to the newly formed cells. For a cell to split into two during meiosis, the duplicated chromosomes must find partners before lining up to get pulled into one of the newly formed cells. Chromosomes having more than one potential partner will be unequally represented in the resulting sex cell. Therefore, none of the gametes will be capable of producing a zygote. In fact, human zygotes will spontaneously abort if they contain more than two copies of the chromosome set. Since only a few plant species have sex chromosomes, many polyploid plant species survive.

Bread Wheat

Plant polyploids are often vigorous and have large fruit. Common bread wheat (*Triticum aestivum*), which is part of many of our lunches, is a polyploid plant (Figure 4.1). Bread wheat has evolved by the combination of genetic material from three different wheat species. The process of mixing chromosomes across species is called hybridization and occurs either in nature or through breeding programs, as is the case with the seedless watermelon. Scientists have found what they believe to be ancient ancestors of modern wheat in the Middle East. Originally, two ancient diploid species came together 8,000 years ago, during the beginning of agriculture, to form the first tetraploid hybrid. This new species hybridized with another ancient diploid to form the modern **hexaploid** species with six sets of chromosomes (*hexa* meaning "six"). The resulting wheat hybrid contains the complete set of chromosomes from three separate species, which provides the plant with many beneficial traits.

Polyploidy and Sterility

Like polyploid animals, polyploid plants are often reproductively sterile. Two examples of successful sterile polyploid plants are seedless watermelons and bananas. Both are triploid, meaning that they have three sets of chromosomes. Chromosome imbalance during meiosis leads to abortion of unusable gametes, which prevents fertilization and subsequent seed formation (Figure 4.2). Consequently, seedless bananas are reproduced vegetatively, meaning that cuttings from young banana trees are planted to form new trees. Seedless watermelons need

Figure 4.1 Common bread wheat (*Triticum aestivum*) is a polyploid plant. Bread wheat has evolved by the combination of genetic material from three different wheat species, providing the plant with many beneficial traits.

to be re-created each time by hybridization to make more triploid seeds. They also require pollination by a fertile diploid relative in order to set fruit.

Polyploidy in Animals

The condition of polyploidy is rare in animals, but it exists in some species such as the grass-eating carp. In animal polyploids, reproduction is impossible because of a chromosomal imbalance in the reproductive cells. Therefore, just like the seedless watermelon,

Origin of Bread Wheat

Triticum aestivum, the grass from which flour is made to bake bread, also known as bread wheat, is a modern cultivated polyploid crop and is globally one of the top five most agronomically important. So, what is the origin of bread wheat? Using genetic markers, researchers have found ancient relatives of bread wheat in the Middle East. About 8,000 years ago, two grandparent diploid grass varieties cross-fertilized to form a hybrid variety. The chromosomes of the hybrid offspring spontaneously doubled to form a tetraploid plant. Then, the new tetraploid was crossed to another diploid species, producing plants with three different sets of chromosomes. The chromosomes of this triple hybrid variety then went through a duplication event, creating the hexaploid bread wheat.

For many years, there has been a debate among archaeologists and plant geneticists over how the ancient hybridization occurred. One question is: Were the ancestral grasses crossed by humans or nature? Many scientists believe that 8,000 years ago was too early in civilization to be practicing agriculture. Thus, these scientists theorize that the hybridization occurred through natural cross-fertilization. However, the traits found in modern bread wheat are so beneficial to agriculture that random cross-fertilization seems out of the question. The group of scientists on the other side of the debate believe that humans conducted the first crosses in one of the earliest events of recognized agriculture.

Regardless of the way in which the crossing took place, both schools of thought agree that ancestral grass varieties from the Middle East hybridized to form modern bread wheat.

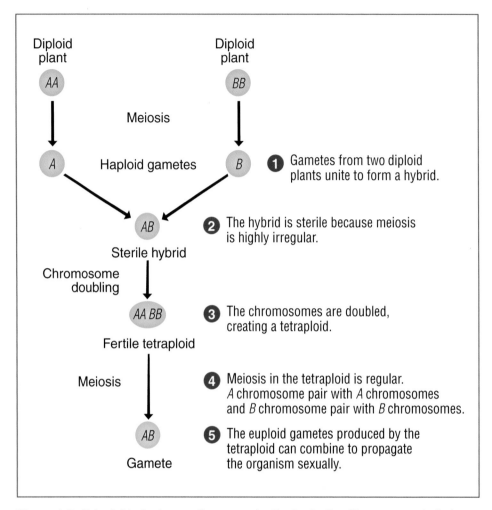

Figure 4.2 Polyploid plants are often reproductively sterile. Chromosome imbalance during meiosis leads to abortion of unusable gametes, which prevents fertilization and subsequent seed formation.

the fish can be reproduced only by mating the two original parent species. The usual type of animal polyploid is a triploid, like the grass-eating carp and the South American turtle. Dr. John W. Bickham of Texas A & M University wrote an article about the triploid turtle discovery, which was published in the scientific journal *Science* in 1985. The triploid variety of the turtle,

Platemys platycephala, can be found in Surinam. Polyploid animals also have been used to perform environmentally friendly cleanup. In Mississippi and other southern states, triploid carp (fish with sharp teeth) are released into marshes to cut the overgrown grass. The triploid carp generate useless reproductive cells because the chromosomes undergo unequal distribution during meiosis. Some gametes will get extra chromosomes and others fewer, creating much variation in the gene dosage in these reproductive cells. Being reproductively sterile prevents the fish from overpopulating the waters.

An exciting article by Dr. Milton Gallardo, which was published in the scientific journal *Nature* in 1999, reported a polyploid mammal. The polyploid mammal discovered is a red viscacha rat, *Tympanoctomys barrerae,* that is found in the South American desert. This rat is much larger than related species from the same area; the liver, for example, is much bigger in the red viscacha. This rat, which is a tetraploid, has twice the DNA content in each of its cells than related species. The extra DNA makes cells larger in mammals, like in plants. One might think that the mammalian fertilized egg should not develop due to the imbalance of the sex chromosomes. There is missing DNA, however, in the tetraploid rat, which is probably the reason for the zygote's survival. Since the chromosome number is not an exact multiple of the number in the basic set, these organisms are not true polyploids; rather, they are **aneuploids** (*aneu* meaning "not true").

MATHEMATICS AND CHROMOSOME NUMBER

One way to understand and distinguish chromosome number in polyploids, diploids, and haploids is to compare a diploid plant (two chromosome sets) to a tetraploid plant (four chromosome sets). The formula for the number of chromosomes, which is represented by the letter *N*, in a sporophytic (spore-producing) cell of a *diploid* organism is $2n = 2x = N$ chromosomes. In this formula, the lower-case n represents the number of chromosomes in reproductive (gametic) cells. Thus, "2n" is the chromosome number in the non-reproductive (somatic) cells. The letter x stands for the number of chromosomes in a complete set, or the monoploid (*mono* meaning "one"). In a gametophytic (gamete-producing) cell, the formula is n = x = N/2 chromosomes. A tetraploid species would have 2n = 4x = N chromosomes in the sporophyte and n = 2x = N/2 in the gametophyte. Thus, we can see that the terms *2n* and *n* mean the same thing whether one is discussing a diploid or polyploid; it is the number before x that changes depending on the organism's ploidy level. By multiplying the monoploid number by the ploidy level, we get N, or the total number of all of the chromosomes in the given cell type.

To illustrate this point, let us revisit the common bread wheat, *Triticum aestivum*. Bread wheat is a hexaploid, meaning it has six sets of chromosomes in each somatic cell. In bread wheat, seven chromosomes total one complete chromosome set. Hence, in the formula for determining chromosome number, the term x would equal seven. For the sporophytic (somatic) cells, the formula representing this diploid form is 2n = 6x = 42 chromosomes in each cell nucleus. For gametophytic (reproductive) cells, which are haploid, the formula is n = 3x = 21 chromosomes, or three sets, in each nucleus.

Other Chromosome Characteristics

Finding a polyploid human would be an extremely rare occurrence due to complications in meiosis that likely would result in a genetically unbalanced zygote. There are conditions in which humans have altered chromosome numbers, but they are not polyploid. In these cases, the chromosome number is not divisible by the basic number of chromosomes in the set. As stated earlier, this condition is called aneuploidy. Aneuploidy can refer to either additional or less chromosomes than the number found in normal **euploids** (*eu* meaning "true"). In humans, aneuploidy leads to developmental abnormalities such as Down syndrome, Turner syndrome, and Klinefelter syndrome. All of these syndromes are evidenced by growth defects and, often, mental retardation.

Datura stramonium, or Jimson weed, is an example of aneuploidy in plants. *D. stramonium* exhibits **trisomy**, which means it has three copies of one chromosome and two copies of all the rest. There are twelve different *Datura* trisomics, one for each chromosome. Plant aneuploids, like the trisomic *D. stramonium*, display different phenotypes, depending on which chromosome is tripled. The seed pods, for example, vary in size among trisomic *Datura*. In any case, all twelve different *Datura* aneuploids survive to become adult plants. Therefore, plants show a much better ability than humans to deal with genetic "shuffling." Where human development is programmed and follows predetermined patterns of cell division and differentiation (specialization), plant development is dynamic in terms of abilities to process genetic material, thereby allowing plants to adapt to a wider variety of environmental conditions.

Many wild species of plants are polyploid, which accounts for the tremendous amount of genetic material available in the wild relatives of cultivated crops. The genetic diversity of wild plant species will be discussed in later chapters focusing on conservation and plant disease resistance.

5 The Diversity of Plants:
Nature's Palette of Genes

The principles of ecological succession bear importantly
on the relationships between man and nature.

— Eugene P. Odum

GENETIC CONSERVATION

In the 1920s, Nicolai Ivanovich Vavilov, a renowned Russian plant breeder, theorized that the origins of modern cultivated crops were rich with genetic diversity and had wild crop relatives that harbored an abundance of important genetic information. Wild species have been tapped by plant breeders through time and have yielded useful genes for related cultivated species. Vavilov recognized the importance of wild species of cultivated crops and the need to look to centers of origin for genetic variability.

Ex situ and *In situ* Conservation

Early in the plant genetics industry, there was a push to collect as many relatives of cultivated crops as possible and to store these samples in **germplasm** collection facilities in various locations (Figure 5.1). Germplasm refers to any type of plant materials, whether whole plants, seeds, or cuttings, that have the ability to pass on genetic information and can be stored for future use. This method is called *ex situ* conservation because the sample (e.g., plant, seed, cutting, tuber) is taken out of its native habitat and stored and propagated elsewhere. This seemed to be the best way to save the genetic diversity of agronomically important species because the samples, safely stored away in germplasm collection facilities, could be evaluated for new and useful genes when needed. However, many plant breeders argue that *ex situ* conservation is not the ideal way to protect genetic diversity of wild relatives of cultivated crops.

Ex situ germplasm collection involves sampling, transfer, and storage of plant material. This requires intensive prior knowledge of not only the species to be sampled, but also of the methods required to move the sample safely to the storage facility. In addition, an ideal environment that mimics the natural habitat must be created to store the germplasm. The *ex situ* method also involves designation of the area to be protected, management of the ecosystem, and monitoring of the wild

Figure 5.1 Scientists at the Vavilov Plant Industry Institute work with stored plant seeds of various plants. The institute has one of the largest collections of genetic plant stock in the world.

species for any changes in populations or phenotypes. One advantage, however, is that the germplasm collection is readily available to researchers and samples can be uniform.

The other approach to conserving plant genetic resources involves protecting entire habitats or whole ecosystems where the wild species of important crops originated. This method is called *in situ* conservation (*in situ* meaning "in self") because the plants of interest are left undisturbed in their natural environments. By allowing the wild species to reside in their original habitats, the plants are able to grow in their natural climate and to interact with native organisms, thereby enabling the process of evolution to continue to produce new genotypes, or genetic makeups. This method of conservation promotes genetic variability through adaptations by keeping the plants in touch with natural environmental pressures.

With *in situ* conservation, the protected plant species are not removed from their native habitat and, therefore, do not require artificial means to keep them alive (Figure 5.2). The only maintenance needed for *in situ* conservation is management and monitoring of the conservatory. This maintenance, however, goes hand in hand with research on the wild species, as one must be able to monitor immediate changes in the habitat and to address the situation accordingly to reduce the risk of losing any valuable germplasm. On the downside, the goals of conservationists may conflict with those of the native population on whose land the plants may reside. The native population either may not understand the conservation efforts, or simply may not want outsiders claiming their land. This is probably the most dangerous and most costly aspect of the *in situ* conservation method.

There are two ways of carrying out *in situ* conservation. One way is to create a genetic reserve, which is essentially marking off an area in which the wild species grows and protecting it from destruction. The other method is the on-farm approach, where existing fields of the wild crop are in use on farms and the practice simply has to be maintained.

The modern cultivated tomato (**Lycopersicon esculentum**) originated in South America, specifically off the coast between Ecuador and Chile. However, there is no evidence of the use of tomato for food or any other purpose in ancient civilizations of South America. It was not until the tomato was brought over to the Old World (i.e. Europe) that it became the cultivar we eat today. The modern tomato cultivar was later reintroduced into South America and Mexico; therefore, Mexico is considered a secondary center of origin. Hence, the only type of *in situ* conservation method to be used for tomato would be a genetic reserve. Since there were no traditional farming practices in place for tomato in South America, the on-farm approach would not apply.

Figure 5.2 Protected plant species are not removed from their native habitat with *in situ* conservation. The only maintenance needed for *in situ* conservation is management and monitoring of the conservatory. This scientist is studying a mangrove forest in Thailand.

Many wild species of the genus *Lycopersicon* exist and thrive in environmental extremes throughout the Andean region and the Galapagos Islands. These species can be found in a range of habitats—from places that get up to 5 meters (about 16.5 feet) of rainfall annually to the shores of the Pacific Ocean where the plants are continuously sprayed by salt water and are grown in salty soil. In addition to these very wet habitats, they also can be found in drought-prone conditions. The ability to grow under these conditions alludes to the genetic variability of these species and, thus, the value of conserving them. Another wild relative of the cultivated tomato, named *L. esculentum* variety *cerasiforme*, can tolerate high temperatures and humidity and is able to resist fungal **pathogens**. *L. pennellii* and *L. chilense* are two wild varieties that contain drought-resistant genes. *L. pimpinellifolium* and *L. hirsutum*, two other wild tomato varieties, both harbor genes conferring resistance to many pathogens. The Galapagos Islands tomato, or *L. cheesmanii*, can thrive in soil containing high salt concentrations. The most genetically variable wild relative of tomato is *L. peruvianum*, which is resistant to many plant pests. As one can see, the wild relatives of tomato are invaluable sources of genetic diversity that can be harnessed to maintain tomato as a viable agricultural crop. Since genetic diversity comes about through environmental selection pressures, many important genes may be lost if the only conservation efforts were through *ex situ* methods that take the plants out of the natural surroundings.

GENETIC DIVERSITY

The climate in western coastal South America is much different than that of Davis, California, and Geneva, New York, where the two major U.S. tomato germplasm collections are located. Because of the differences in the environments (most notably, the climate and the surrounding organisms), plants in the *ex situ* germplasm collections are affected by different selection pressures than those plants that reside in their places of origin. The lack of diversity in the fields where the *ex situ* germplasm collection is spread will slow the rate at which novel traits evolve; in other words, there will be a "freezing" of evolution. In contrast, an *in situ* germplasm remains in contact with pests and pathogens, enabling the plant to adapt to changes in plant parasites. The plants that survive in the environment of the *ex situ* collections will adapt to these environments due to the small population size but will also experience genetic drift, forcing them ultimately to become a homozygous population of unvarying genotypes. This can lead to major problems if, in the future, plant breeders need to exploit germplasm collections for new genes that can combat emerging crop pests and other environmental pressures, such as high salt and drought. Wild relatives are the source of genetic diversity because they contend with a vast array of other plant species and organisms. From neighboring trees to insects pollinating wild crops, all organisms in a natural habitat contribute to evolving genetic diversity.

Not only does *in situ* conservation of wild crop relatives maintain genetic diversity, it also ensures that, by protecting the whole

National Plant Germplasm System

Keeping collections of plant material for conservation of species has been a practice of plant breeders for over a century. Seeds can be stored for long periods, provided the correct climactic conditions (temperature and humidity) are met. Other parts of plants such as roots and shoot cuttings can also be stored and used to propagate more plants either to bulk up the material or to refresh the collection with younger plants. Plant material kept in collections is called germplasm. Most germplasm collections are stored in climate-controlled rooms far from their native habitats. This method of storing plant collections in a controlled environment is called *ex situ* (pronounced: "eks see chew") conservation. *Ex situ* is a Latin phrase that means "outside of self." In essence, the plants are collected and kept in a place that is outside of their natural habitats. The United States has a large collection of plant samples that can be searched and browsed online (see page 116). Having a few central repositories for plant materials makes it easy to request and receive samples; this is one of the advantages of having a germplasm collection. Plant materials from the National Plant Germplasm System are available free to academic and other noncommercial researchers.

ecosystem, the wild species does not become extinct. In contrast, *ex situ* conservation protects only a sample taken from a natural habitat. This does not prevent the destruction of that habitat, which would make the germplasm **accession** the only surviving representative of that species if destruction of the habitat were to occur. If this were the case, the crop ultimately could face genetic erosion and could fall victim to environmental pressures that would eventually render the crop unable to be economically and practically cultivated.

Tissue Culture in Germplasm Collections

In many germplasm collections, samples are in the form of seeds, which can be easily and safely stored for long periods in controlled environments. However, some plant species never or rarely make seeds or their seeds cannot withstand long-term storage. In cases like these, scientists must rely on different methods of maintaining a species in such a way that it can be grown to full size at a future time or sent to researchers who want to study it. One widely practiced way of keeping these types of plants in germplasm collections is through the use of tissue culture. Tissue culture involves the growth of a small part of a plant, for example the root or the shoot, in a nutrient-rich artificial medium. The plant tissue can be induced to form other organs and a full plant by applying appropriate hormones to the medium. In this way, only one specimen may be necessary for a single germplasm collection because multiple pieces of the plant can be grown in multiple containers like test tubes for easy and widespread distribution. Tissue culture is especially advantageous for plants that propagate vegetatively, such as potatoes. Since the tuber of a potato is the tissue from which new plants sprout, simply taking slices of potato tubers and putting them on a growth medium will result in a new plant. Another advantage is that all tissues grown from the same plant will have identical genotypes, thereby eliminating unwanted variation in samples. This is important when different researchers want to compare their genetic studies.

Plant and Animal Diversity

Genetic diversity can be seen in members throughout the plant kingdom, perhaps more so than in the animal kingdom. Since humans are classified under the animal kingdom, one can make the comparison between plant and animal cells extend to human cells. Plant cells are similar to human cells, but they also differ in many ways. For one, plant cells have cell walls surrounding a plasma membrane, while human cells only have plasma membranes. Cell walls are dynamic structures made of a **cellulose** matrix, which gives plants the ability to grow tall and to support branches. Also unlike human cells, plant cells contain specialized organelles called chloroplasts. Earlier, we learned that the genetic material needed for proper development, in both plants and humans, is in the genome, which is located in the nucleus, but other specialized genomes exist.

For plants and humans, there are separate genomes in the organelles known as mitochondria. Mitochondria are the "powerhouses" of the cell because this is where the cell stores and makes energy in the form of ATP, which is used in many processes required to keep the organism alive and growing. Like the mitochondria, chloroplasts also have their own separate genomes. The genes in the chloroplast genome are involved in carrying out the processes of photosynthesis, or the conversion of light energy to chemical energy in the form of starch. One interesting finding of chloroplast genomes is that they seem to be inherited in non-Mendelian ways. That is, the genomes of chloroplasts are found only in the female gametes and, thus, carry only traits of the female parent plant. One can see evidence of the variation in chloroplast genomes in plants whose leaves are multicolored, such as the *Mirabilis* plant.

6 Genetically Controlled Processes

The tree is more than first a seed, then a stem,
then a living trunk, and then dead timber.
The tree is a slow, enduring force straining to win the sky.
— Antoine de Saint-Exupéry

Genetically Controlled Processes

SIGNAL RECEPTORS

When a plant experiences a dramatic change, for example in temperature, this is a type of stress. Plants deal with different stresses by sending signals from their outermost cells (for example, the cells on the surface of a leaf or stem) to the rest of the plant in order to prepare the plant for the stress. The signals are usually in the form of small molecules that interact with proteins, which receive and send the signal to further locations. Protein-based signaling pathways like this usually involve enzymes called **kinases**. Kinases are specialized enzymes that add phosphate molecules to other proteins. The addition of the phosphate molecule causes a change in the protein's physical properties, like its shape. This change then leads to interactions with other proteins that recognize the changed protein form.

Before a gene's mRNA can be translated into amino acids, the DNA must be transcribed by RNA polymerases within the nucleus of the cell. Gene expression is regulated following a series of signaling events orchestrated through kinases from the plasma membrane to inside the nucleus. In many signaling pathways, there are **receptors**—specialized proteins or parts of proteins situated on the outside of the cell that stretch beyond the plasma membrane and cell wall—that can perceive signaling molecules from other neighboring cells or even signals from outside of the plant.

Hormones belong to a group of signaling molecules that are constantly being perceived by receptors. Plant hormones such as **auxin**, **cytokinin**, **brassinosteroid**, and **ethylene** are known to have roles in growth and development.

Auxin

Auxin has been implicated in almost all facets of growth and development. One well-known effect of auxin on plant growth is **apical dominance**, or vertical growth of the primary shoot with reduced side branches. When auxin is sprayed onto a plant, the plants show increased height and decreased branching when compared to plants that were not sprayed.

Cytokinin

Cytokinin, like auxin, has roles in various growth processes. There is evidence that cytokinin and auxin play competing roles in certain growth processes. Studies in the laboratory have shown that undifferentiated cells, called **callus**, can be induced to differentiate into roots or shoots by adding auxin or cytokinin to the nutrient supply.

Brassinosteroid

Brassinosteroid is a hormone that is involved in many aspects of plant growth and development, from leaf formation to fertility. Much work in the past decade on the brassinosteroid pathway has focused on the genetic interactions. At least three different brassinosteroid receptors have been identified in *Arabidopsis*, as have several downstream (i.e., farther down the signal chain) proteins. The brassinosteroid recognition pathway, with its multiple surface receptors and intermediate players, is very complex. Researchers have not yet found all of the pieces in the puzzle of the brassinosteroid pathway; more knowledge will come as new results shed light on how plant cells communicate within and among each other.

Ethylene

Among other effects, the plant hormone ethylene is most notably known to induce fruit ripening. The first plant hormone receptor, an ethylene receptor, was identified and cloned by Dr. Anthony Bleecker. This receptor protein has a kinase domain, so it is likely that it both perceives the ethylene signal and sends it along to the next component in the pathway. There are several ethylene receptors known in *Arabidopsis*. Like brassinosteroid, the ethylene pathway also has not been completely demystified. Science is ongoing, as long as there are questions still to be asked.

MODELS OF TRANSDUCTION

Auxin, cytokinin, brassinosteroid, and ethylene are being investigated thoroughly by researchers worldwide. Many of the protein players in the brassinosteroid pathway have been discovered, and the pathway appears to follow a network of kinase interactions—from the receptor kinase at the top of the chain on the plasma membrane through other receptor-activated and **mitogen**-activated kinase cascades to the transcription factors in the nucleus. A mitogen is any molecule that interacts with another molecule or protein based on its structure.

For signaling pathways, plant pathogens are a major source of external **stimuli**, which are molecules from outside of the plant. Many plant pathogens have molecules that enter a plant cell upon infection or that interact with a specific receptor, which transmits a signal to alert the cell of an attack. The receptor can be a stand-alone protein or can be part of a larger protein that may have an **enzymatic** portion inside the cell (Figure 6.1). In either case, the receptor relays the signal by some action, such as a change in shape, or through a transfer of atoms, like an electrical current. Inside the cell, in the space called the cytoplasm, there are more proteins associated with the signaling pathway, which interact with the signal from the first enzyme of the cascade (Figure 6.2). The signal is transferred from one kinase to the next, like a domino effect, moving from the perimeter of the cell to inside the nucleus, without losing strength. In most cases, the signal from the outer edge of the cell is amplified on its way to the nucleus. Signaling pathways that increase the signal strength from the receptor to the nucleus usually recruit multiple molecules of cytoplasmic proteins to interact with the initial enzyme, thereby distributing the same signal over more space.

Gene Regulation

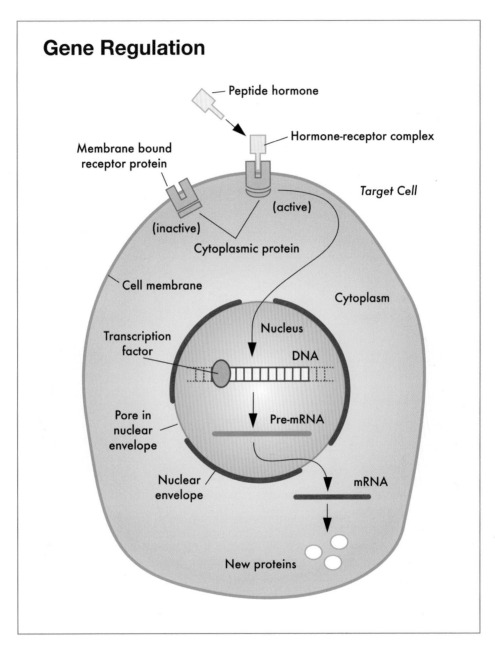

Figure 6.1 This large protein receptor has an enzymatic portion inside the cell. In this diagram, the hormone-receptor complex activates a cytoplasmic protein that induces a transcription factor to bind to DNA and stimulates transcription that transports mRNA to the cytoplasm.

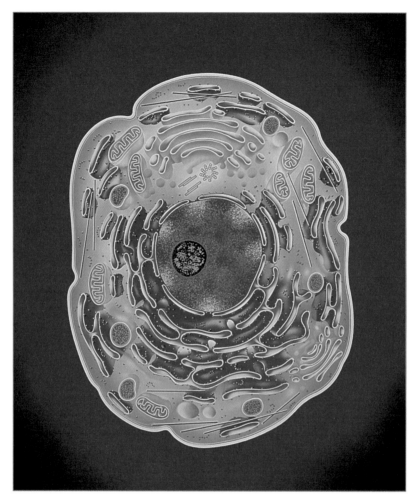

Figure 6.2 The cytoplasm surrounds the inside of the cell (purple). Ribosomes (red dots), which are the sites of protein synthesis, are located within the cytoplasm. In the cytoplasm, there are more proteins associated with the signaling pathway, which interact with the signal from the first enzyme of the cascade.

Gene Expression

Inside the nucleus, there are proteins that bind DNA called transcription factors. When activated, these **DNA-binding proteins (DBPs)** latch on to (or let go of, if already attached) the regulatory region of a gene after a signal is received. The regulatory region of a gene can be either an enhancer or a silencer of gene expression. Regulatory regions can reside at the end, in the middle, or at the beginning of a gene sequence. Remember, the sequence before the mRNA coding region of a gene's DNA sequence is called the promoter. Initiating transcription of the gene into mRNA, the promoter is bound by transcription factor proteins that are then bound by **RNA polymerases**, which are enzymes that "read" the DNA sequence and make a complementary RNA strand. Depending on the cue from the signal, a transcription factor either will enable or disable the production of more RNA messages for a given gene by either allowing or hindering the binding of RNA polymerases to the promoter. The increase or decrease in mRNA that is sent out of the nucleus to the cytoplasm will result in an increase or decrease of protein products for that gene. Ultimately, the number of protein products that are available for the cellular process affected by the signaling pathway will determine the outcome of the initial signal. In a **regulatory** system, cellular processes are kept in **equilibrium** (balanced) through signals picked up from outside the plant or from adjacent cells that are continuously delivered to the nucleus, where transcription occurs. In essence, a plant cell is always "in tune" with its environment and its hormonal state by controlling physiological processes with gene expression.

Control of protein number not only occurs at the step of producing mRNA, but also involves degrading (breaking down) whole proteins when their number is too much. The process of targeting a protein for degradation is called **ubiquitination**. The basic mode of protein ubiquitination involves "tagging" a protein with an ubiquitin, which is another protein that attracts protein-cutting enzymes, called **proteases**, to the location. In the process of ubiquitination, the amino acids of the peptide chain are separated and reused for future protein needs. In this way, the plant can quickly regulate the protein numbers in the cell while also recycling the parts of the unused proteins.

Phytochromes

Plants and humans share similar methods of transferring signals within and between cells. This is a major part of the physiological process that occurs in all organisms, including bacteria, plants, insects, and animals. However, plants have other, genetically controlled physiological processes that are not found in humans or animal cells. One major process plants carry out that humans do not is photosynthesis. In nature, plants rely on sunlight as a source of energy, and they make proteins that recognize the intensity and the color of the light to which they are exposed. In addition to photosynthesis, light is an important input for other plant processes, including **photoperiodism**, which is the plant's ability to respond to day length, and **photomorphogenesis**, which is the plant's growth response to light.

Sunlight is a mixture, or spectrum, of different colors of light. Light comes in the form of waves, and different colors are made by varying the wavelengths. **Phytochromes** are plant proteins that recognize and respond to light in the red and far-red regions of the spectrum. Red light peaks at a wavelength of about 660 nanometers (nm) and far-red at about 730 nm. (A nanometer is a unit of length equal to one-billionth of a meter, which is one million times smaller than the head of a pin.) In flowering plants, there are five different phytochromes that affect different biological activities when activated by red or far-red light. Phytochrome proteins exist in two forms, depending on what type of light is shining on the plant. If the plant is hit by red light, then the phytochrome responsible for detecting red light is degraded and the type that detects far-red light is produced, and vice versa. In essence, there is always a dynamic ratio of phytochrome for red (Pr) and phytochrome for far-red (Pfr) light (Figure 6.3).

One biological process that depends on the intensity of red versus far-red light is flowering. Some plants get the signal to flower in short days or long nights, and other plants flower in the opposite conditions. Since red light is "seen" by the plant at

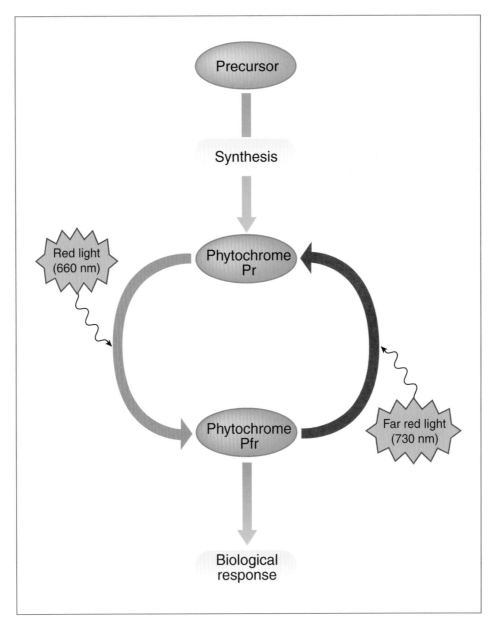

Figure 6.3 Phytochrome exists in two forms: Pr (red light) and Pfr (far-red light), depending on what type of light is shining on the plant. If the plant is hit by red light, then the phytochrome responsible for detecting red light is degraded and the type that detects far-red light is produced. There is always a dynamic ratio of phytochrome for Pr and Pfr light.

dusk (just before sundown), the Pr form is degraded and the Pfr form is made. When enough Pfr has been produced, an unknown intermediate substance triggers the expression of transcription factors that "turn on" the genes involved in initiating flowering. Because the amount of Pfr protein in a plant is critical for inducing flowering, a specific minimum length of time needed to make the Pfr must pass after sundown. Plant geneticists have shown that a long-night plant that has been in darkness for several hours can be prevented from flowering with just a flash of red light. This illustrates the sensitivity of the phytochrome-flowering time system.

Self-incompatibility and the S-locus Receptor

Nature has incorporated plants with the need to cross-fertilize by making self-fertilization impossible. This characteristic is called **self-incompatibility**. In a self-incompatible relationship, pollen cannot grow a tube through the style to the ovary; hence fertilization does not occur. The reason for a plant to be self-incompatible may not be obvious at first, but when one looks at the diversity of plants and the need to survive in an environment in which a plant cannot escape, the reason becomes clear. By making some plants **outcross**, or cross-fertilize with other varieties of the same species, nature has implemented a way for these plants to continually hybridize, thereby keeping the genetic pool diversified. The genetics underlying self-incompatibility have been studied extensively and while some players have been identified, research in this area is still ongoing.

There are actually two types of self-incompatibility. One type is called sporophytic self-incompatibility (SSI) and the other is gametophytic self-incompatibility (GSI). Both types have a genotype of alleles in a specific region of the genome called the **S-locus**. In SSI, the genotype of the sporophyte, the diploid tissue of the plant from which the pollen arises, determines whether the pollen grain will germinate on the stigma. If the genotype of at least one of the two S-locus alleles from each of the pollen-bearing and pistil-containing flowers matches, then growth of the pollen tube down the style is prevented through SSI. In GSI, the genotype of the single S-locus allele in the haploid pollen grain must match either of the two alleles of the diploid pistil for pollen tube germination and fertilization of the female egg cell to be blocked.

7 Identifying Functions of Genes

Those who contemplate the beauty of the earth find reserves of strength that will endure as long as life lasts.
— Rachel Carson

Identifying Functions of Genes

MUTANT GENERATION

One way scientists try to figure out possible functions of genes is by creating mutant plants that are somehow altered in their DNA coding sequence. There are several methods of mutating plants, including chemicals, X-rays, and genetic engineering. The last method, which inserts DNA into a random place in the plant genome, is intended to stop a plant from transcribing a gene into mRNA, thereby preventing translation to the gene's protein product. This is called a **knockout** mutant because the ability to make the gene product is essentially removed from the plant. However, the random insertion of DNA in the genome can result in the gene being merely altered. In this case, the mutant plant can still make a protein product, but it will be deficient or work differently than the wild type version of the protein.

Gene Function

Let's look at a situation where mutant plants would be used to understand gene function. A plant scientist **hypothesizes** that by disrupting a gene there would be a phenotype, or characteristic of the plant, that would be different from a normal (unaltered) plant of the same variety. For example, if a mutant plant shows asymmetrically shaped leaves, then the scientist may deduce that the normal function of the gene is to ensure equal growth on both sides of the leaf's midvein (i.e., the tube-like structure running lengthwise from the base of the leaf to the tip). Without the properly functioning gene, the leaf development is abnormal. With this hypothesis in mind, the scientist would carry out experiments to prove the hypothesis; in this case, the scientist may measure the size and number of cells on both sides of the leaf. Ultimately, to prove that a gene is responsible for a proposed function, the scientist would carry out a **complementation** experiment. In a complementation experiment, a wild type copy, or form, of the gene in question is introduced into the mutant plant using genetic engineering methods, much like the way the plant was mutated in the first place. If the **transgenic**, or genetically engineered, progeny plants of the transformed mutant plant have normal leaf shape, then the introduced gene is the same as the gene that was disrupted in the mutant plant. This method of figuring out functions of genes by knocking out specific genes and looking for deviations from wild type plants is called **reverse genetics.** The term *reverse* is used because the scientist already knows the sequence of the gene and wants to find a function, essentially working "backward" from how geneticists worked before the days of genome sequencing. Genome sequencing will be explored further in chapter 9.

The opposite of reverse genetics is called **forward genetics.** In forward genetics, a population of plants is mutagenized, creating disruptions randomly throughout the genome. This effectively leads to many different phenotypes observed in the mutant varieties. A scientist's job in forward genetics is to choose a mutant plant with a phenotype and figure out the gene responsible for the phenotype. This method is more time consuming than reverse genetics because it involves a process called **mapping,** which is akin to creating a treasure map without knowing anything about the treasure. In this analogy, the gene responsible for the lost function is the treasure. The scientist will rely on specific sequences of DNA called **markers** to narrow down the location within the genome of the gene responsible for the function of interest.

GENE MAPPING

The first step when isolating a gene is to create a **mapping population,** which is a collection of plants that come from the same two parent plants. A mapping population is a cross between a mutant plant and a closely related but different variety of plant. The plant that is crossed with the mutant must have enough differences within its genome that they can be used to distinguish between the two varieties. By knowing which markers correlate to which parent variety of the mapping population and where these markers reside in the genome, one can detect crossover events within the plants of the mapping population. By relating these crossover events, or **recombinations** that occur when the genetic material of one parent mixes with that of the other, to the phenotype of the offspring plant (either mutant or normal), one can see whether the phenotype is **linked**, meaning attached during meiosis, to a specific marker. When a phenotype is linked to a marker on the same chromosome, the location of the gene can be narrowed down even further, which is a process called **fine mapping**.

Web-based Resources for Genomics

Advances in genetics of plants, animals, fruit flies, and microorganisms have led to the accumulation of a lot of information within the research community. Almost simultaneously, computer programming and Internet technology have made leaps and bounds in the past decade. Modern genetic research requires enormous databases to store data, like DNA sequences, mutant phenotypes, and literature associated with particular experiments. The National Center for Biological Information (NCBI) has several databases available for searching on the web. From the NCBI homepage (*http://www.ncbi.nlm.nih.gov*) visitors can search for scientific articles using the PubMed database, look for information about a single gene across multiple databases, or link to other resources within the NCBI website.

One popular page to visit at NCBI is called the BLAST page. BLAST, which stands for Basic Local Alignment Search Tool, is a way of comparing genetic information using computer-driven mathematical formulas. With BLAST, a researcher can input a sequence (either DNA or amino acid) and search for close matches to sequences in the database. The sequences that are matched are then returned to the user in a list from most to least similar. A DNA input sequence can be translated to an amino acid sequence and vice versa. One can search for protein matches using DNA or amino acid input sequences. Likewise, an amino acid sequence can be used to search a DNA database.

Once the location of a gene is narrowed down to a stretch of the genome that can be fully sequenced, the geneticist can create a list of candidate genes for complementation analysis, based on the sequences obtained from that small region. The next step is to clone all of the candidate genes into vectors, which are used to insert the gene into the genome of the mutant plant. Scientists employ a certain species of bacterium called **Agrobacterium tumefaciens** to infect the plant cell and to release the gene vector to the nucleus where it is randomly inserted in the genome. Found in the wild, *Agrobacterium* is actually a disease-causing bacterium for some plants and is responsible for crown gall, a disease in some trees (Figure 7.1). The symptom of crown gall disease is the formation of tumors on the base of a tree. The bacterium inserts into the plant genome a piece of DNA called **transfer DNA** (**T-DNA**) that has sequences for tumor-causing genes, thus making the plant create its own tumors. The *Agrobacterium* that is used by plant geneticists to transform plants, however, has been engineered so that the harmful, tumor-causing genes are gone. The T-DNA in the bacterium resides on a circular piece of DNA called a **plasmid**, which is separate from the bacterial genome. Since the original T-DNA of the wild type *Agrobacterium* is missing from the engineered form, the plant scientist can insert any piece of DNA in this position. By using standard molecular biology techniques, transformation of the *Agrobacterium* with the gene of interest is quickly and efficiently performed (Figure 7.2). Once it has been verified that the correct DNA piece is in the bacterial plasmid, which is done through use of molecular biology techniques, the *Agrobacterium* can be prepared for plant transformation.

Materials for Plant Transformation

Arabidopsis is a good example to use when illustrating plant transformation because it has a high-transformation efficiency and has been transformed by researchers for over a decade. The

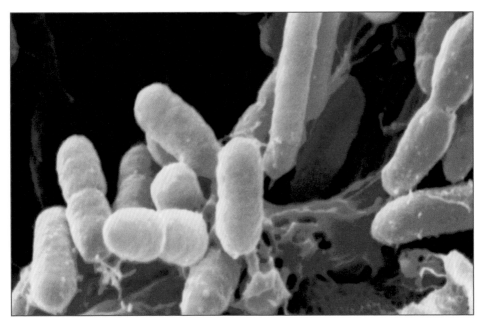

Figure 7.1 *Agrobacterium tumefaciens* is a disease-causing bacterium for some plants, such as the damaged tobacco plant shown here. *Agrobacterium* is responsible for crown gall disease, but it is also being used to introduce genes during genetic manipulation.

most common method of transforming *Arabidopsis* is by the floral dip. In this procedure, the *Agrobacterium* cells are collected and resuspended in a special buffer solution, and the flower buds of the plant are submerged in the bacteria-containing liquid for a few minutes. By immersing the flower buds in a solution of *Agrobacterium*, the gametes become the target cells for T-DNA insertion. Since gametes come together to make seeds, the introduced DNA will be passed on to the zygotes, and the plants that grow from these seeds will be mutant. Of course, not all of the gametes in the flower receive the T-DNA, so antibiotic selection is used to select for those seeds that are mutant. In the engineered T-DNA, an antibiotic-resistant gene resides that allows plant geneticists to grow the seeds from a "dipped" plant on a growth medium that contains the corresponding antibiotic. The

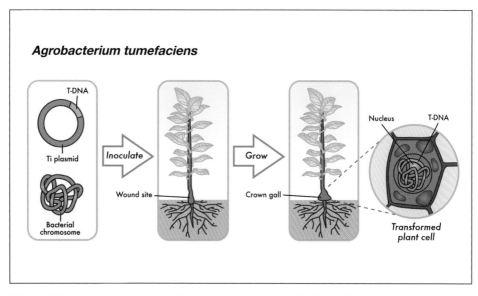

Agrobacterium tumefaciens

Figure 7.2 *Agrobacterium* has been engineered to eliminate harmful, tumor-causing genes. The T-DNA in the bacterium resides on a circular piece of DNA called a plasmid. Since the original T-DNA of the wild-type *Agrobacterium* is missing from the engineered form, the plant scientist can insert any piece of DNA in this position. Once the correct DNA piece is in the bacterial plasmid, the *Agrobacterium* can be prepared for plant transformation.

seedlings that survive after germination and display normal growth are the potential mutants and are saved for further characterization. Because gametes are haploid and zygotes are diploid, there will be only one copy of the introduced DNA sequence in the seedlings of the first transformed generation, or T0. In other words, the selected seedlings will be heterozygous for the inserted T-DNA. In order to see the phenotype of a recessive allele, the flowers of the T0 generation are self-fertilized. The progeny, or T1 generation, seeds with the affected allele will segregate with a ratio of 1:2:1 for homozygous mutant, heterozygous, and homozygous wild type. This is where *Arabidopsis* is beneficial as a model system; one can let the surviving seedlings grow to adult plants, make flowers, self-fertilize, and set seed without doing much more than keeping the plants watered.

8 Agricultural Advances

A seed hidden in the heart of an apple is an orchard invisible.

— Welsh Proverb

Agricultural Advances

CROP SELECTION AND PLANT QUALITY

With world population increasing and farmland becoming less abundant, the need for high-yielding crops is of utmost importance. Plant researchers were aware of this need in the 1940s when they developed new varieties of wheat for Mexico. These new wheat varieties were bred to grow shorter to make harvesting by machine easier; shorter varieties do not lodge (fall over), which is a problem associated with traditional taller varieties of wheat. Plant breeders crossed many different types of wheat and looked for improvements in important qualities such as height and grain yield in each generation of hybrids. By selecting the best-looking plants from hybrid populations and crossing these plants to other quality varieties, breeders ended up with a variety of wheat that had the exact qualities they needed (Figure 8.1).

The name given to the improved quality of plants that result from out-crossing is **hybrid vigor**. Along with hybrid vigor comes the idea of **heterosis.** Heterosis refers to the genetic diversity of a plant's genome that results from cross-fertilization with other varieties of the same species. The effectiveness of heterosis is unclear, but geneticists speculate that it has to do with keeping the genome dynamic, or always changing. The opposite of hybrid vigor is **inbreeding depression**, which occurs by generation after generation of self-fertilization. Inbreeding depression results in poorer yields and crop quality with each successive generation.

The agricultural crops that are grown worldwide are not the ancient varieties that grew before the time of organized agricultural practices. Modern crops are the result of decades of work by plant breeders. For example, sweet corn has improved not only in sweetness, but also in strength of the stalk and in ability to withstand pests, pathogens, and other environmental factors.

Plant Pathogen Interactions

As far back as the early 1900s, scientists believed that a pathogen,

Figure 8.1 Plant researchers have developed new varieties of wheat for Mexican crops. The center stalk of wheat is a crossbreed of the two stalks on either side.

or causative agent of a disease, "injected" some type of molecule into the plant **host** that, in turn, interacted with a molecule from the plant. Later, it was hypothesized that this interaction led to a signal being sent to the nucleus, where transcription of genes involved in disease defense would be regulated. Now, it has been shown that wild species of cultivated crops contain genes that confer resistance to many plant pathogens. These pathogens can be either pests such as insects and worms, or diseases caused by viruses or bacteria (Figure 8.2). The cultivated potato, for example, has wild relatives that are native to the Andes, a mountain range around the countries of Peru and Chile in South America. This wild potato grows in an environment where there are also many potential pathogens. Today, the biggest problem that affects farmers who grow cultivated potatoes is the loss of crops due to the fungus-like organism called *Phytopthera infestans* (Figure 8.3). This **microorganism** is the cause of the potato disease known as **late blight**; this disease was responsible for the infamous Irish potato famine of the 1840s. The native location of the wild potato in the Andes can become very humid, which is the perfect climate for growing *P. infestans*. Thus, wild potato plants must contend with and resist attacks by predatory neighbors like *P. infestans*. Through genetic mutations that have led to new resistance products, evolution has allowed the wild potato and this pathogen to live side by side.

Spontaneous mutations give rise to new gene sequences that, in turn, can lead to new RNA or protein products. The plants with altered genetic products that can survive the onslaught of neighboring pathogens are the ancestors of the wild species found in the Andes today. Just as wild potatoes have been able to defend themselves against *P. infestans*, the microorganism has been able to overcome host resistance by mutations in the *Phytopthera* genome. These mutations in the pathogen's genome give rise to different genes than the ones that had been recognized by the host plant in earlier generations. So, the

Figure 8.2 Plant pathogens can be either pests such as insects and worms, or diseases caused by viruses or bacteria. Colorado beetles (upper left), the potato leaf hopper (upper right), and flea beetles (upper center) are insects that can affect the potato plant. Viruses and fungi that harm the leaves of a potato plant include the potato leaf roll virus (upper left), late blight fungus (lower left), and early blight fungus (lower right).

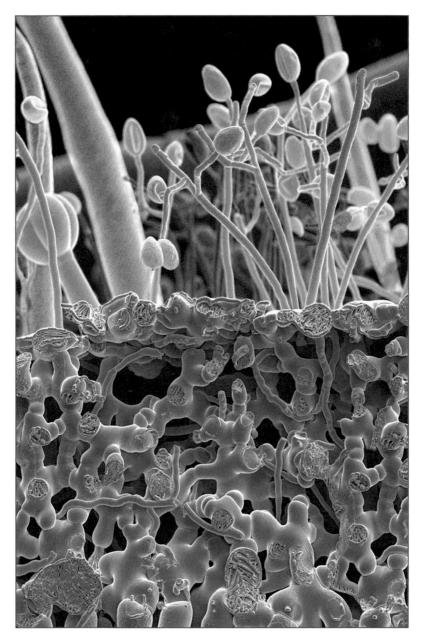

Figure 8.3 This electron micrograph scanning shows a section of a potato leaf infected with potato blight. *Phytopthera infestans* is a microorganism that can cause late blight disease, which was responsible for the Irish potato famine of the 1840s.

battle continues: with each genetic change that the pathogen goes through, the potato counters with a new, resistant gene to recognize the intruding organism.

Gene-for-Gene Resistance

In 1940, the plant geneticist Dr. Harold H. Flor was the first person to officially describe this type of pathogen resistance. Flor's theory, which is called **gene-for-gene resistance,** states that for each pathogen there exists a specific gene product, or **elicitor,** that is unique for a certain plant host. When the pathogen molecule enters a plant cell, it is recognized by a specific gene product, which triggers the resistance mechanism in the plant. Plant pathologists call the gene in the microorganism the **avirulence gene** (*a* meaning "not" and *virulence* referring to the ability to infect) because it is the recognition of this gene product by the host plant that enables disease resistance to occur. The resistant-gene product in the plant is specific to a pathogen's avirulence-gene product. One might ask why a pathogen would evolve to have a gene that allows the potential host to resist it. The reason is that the pathogen did not evolve "knowingly" because evolution occurs through spontaneous mutations and the host plant could have evolved the resistant gene after the pathogen had its avirulence gene.

Elicitor and defense genes are relative to plant and pathogen genotypes, which leads to the idea of **compatible** and **incompatible interactions** between pathogens and hosts. A compatible interaction occurs when a pathogen is able to invade and to infect a host because the plant does not mount any defense. Thus, for the pathogen, the interaction is compatible because it is able to infect the host plant. In an incompatible interaction, the plant's disease resistance mechanism is triggered and the pathogen cannot infect the host. So, if a pathogen does not have a gene product that matches one from the potential host, the pathogen can infect that host successfully without encountering resistance from the plant. This is why the two organisms can co-habitate the same environment and how much of the genetic diversity in plants arises.

Genetic Engineering and Agriculture

Since the onset of the Green Revolution, which used classical plant-breeding methods to introduce favorable traits into important crops, scientists have been experimenting with ways of making the process faster and better. After all, one of the major goals of science is progress. With the birth of genetic engineering, that is using laboratory techniques to manipulate genetic

Origin of Corn

A long-term debate among plant breeders and geneticists has been the origin of modern cultivated corn, also known as maize. There are two hypotheses when it comes to the issue of the corn's origin. The most popular is the teosinte hypothesis, stating that modern corn evolved from a single ancient wild grass called teosinte. The other, proposed in 1938 by Paul Mangelsdorf and Robert Reeves, is the tripartite hypothesis, which states that teosinte is the product of maize crossing with another wild grass, called *Tripsacum,* and is not the progenitor to modern cultivated corn. In 2004, Dr. Mary Eubanks, a Duke University plant geneticist, announced her conclusion from experiments with corn and wild grasses from central and South America that corn is the product of hybridization events between teosinte and *Tripsacum*, also known as gamagrass. Employing modern genetic technology, Dr. Eubanks and her team were able to identify similarities between corn and both teosinte and gamagrass. Her theory partially supports the teosinte hypothesis in that teosinte is viewed as one of the ancient progenitors of corn, but not the sole source. With advances in molecular plant genetics constantly occurring, it may not be long before scientists find evidence to undoubtedly confirm the origin of corn.

material, plant geneticists have been able to introduce many traits to important crops. One such advancement is "Bt corn," an insect-resistant corn variety engineered by Monsanto chemical company. This transgenic corn carries a gene from a bacterium called *Bacillus thuringiensis* (Bt). The bacterial gene, which is expressed in the pollen of corn flowers, codes for a toxin that kills insect larvae when the pollen grains are ingested. Scientists at Monsanto figured out how to insert the foreign, bacterial DNA into corn, which then transcribed and translated the toxin protein by the machinery of the corn plant. This result alone shows the universal nature of the genetic code.

9 Plant Genomics and Beyond

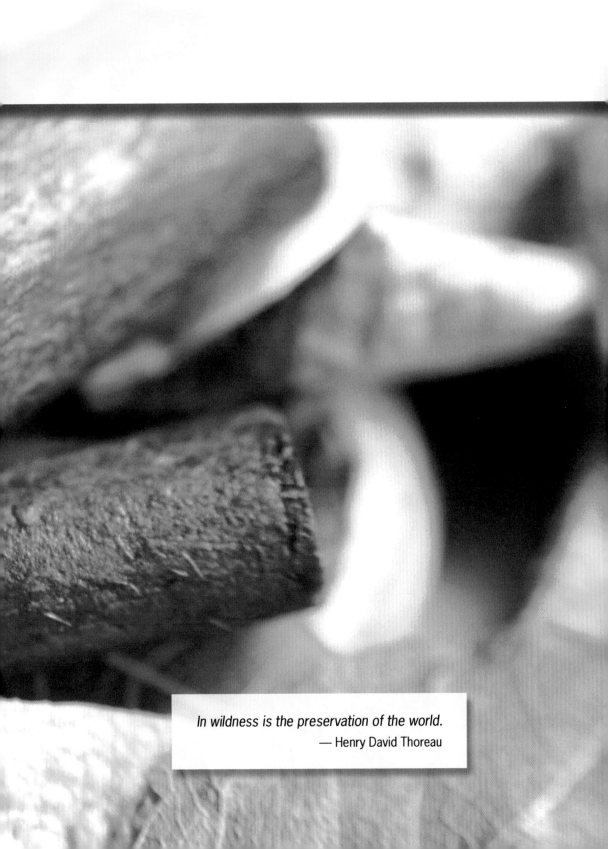

In wildness is the preservation of the world.
— Henry David Thoreau

Plant Genomics and Beyond

ARABIDOPSIS

The small plant from the mustard family, called *Arabidopsis thaliana* (also known as thale cress or mouse-ear cress), has been used as a model plant system for decades. Having been the first plant to have its entire genome sequenced, *Arabidopsis* is a model system for investigating the genetics of development, growth, and environmental interactions of higher plants (Figure 9.1). *Arabidopsis* is easy to grow because it is small and has a fast life cycle (only six weeks from planting a seed to harvesting new seeds). *Arabidopsis* also has a relatively small genome, which makes it easy to find genes of important functions. Currently, the international research community studying *Arabidopsis* has approximately 13,000 members, each working on some aspect of *Arabidopsis*, from growth and development to pathogen and environmental interactions. An organized committee has established the Multinational Coordinated *Arabidopsis thaliana* Functional Genomics Project, which has a 10-year plan to figure out the functions of all 25,000 *Arabidopsis* genes. The project, which started in 2001, has accomplished multiple **annotations**, or revisions, of the genome sequence based on computer-driven sequence analyses and experiments by researchers. This annotation of the genome sequence is important for correctly identifying gene locations, numbers of similar genes, and non-protein coding sequence. Sequenced genomes also allow scientists to evaluate the site of genes and to determine what other genetic information exists near the area of a gene on the chromosome.

Many of the basic biological questions about plants can be addressed and answered using *Arabidopsis* as a model system. For instance, genes that are identical in DNA sequence are called **homologs**; many homologs of *Arabidopsis* genes have been identified in economically important crops, such as rice. This suggests that the resources available for *Arabidopsis* can be used to shed light on plants that are agronomically important on a

Figure 9.1 Thale cress is a flowering plant that has been a model system for investigating the genetics of development, growth, and environmental interactions of higher plants.

global scale. Comparing *Arabidopsis* to rice is like comparing humans to dogs because between each pair there is a high similarity of DNA sequences.

Like the human genome, the *Arabidopsis* genome sequence is providing tools to understand the complex interactions of genes during development and throughout the life of the organism. Plant genome sequences will also help to further bridge the gap between relationships of near and distantly related plant species by methods of sequence analysis. For some genes, it has been shown that gene homologs found in different plant species, such as tomatoes and rice, have similar functions. This link is very useful. Plant scientists can use different plants or model systems to study mechanisms of growth and environmental interaction and then apply that knowledge to other plants of agronomic or economic importance (Figure 9.2).

Comparative Genetics

Using information from the sequenced genome of an organism to relate the organism to other organisms without sequenced genomes is called **comparative genetics**. Because large-scale sequencing projects like whole genome sequencing can be extremely costly, not many big genomes have been sequenced. For this matter, comparative genetics is extremely valuable when assessing genes for important traits that have been identified in the sequenced genome, but not in genomes of other important organisms. Regarding both humans and *Arabidopsis*, comparisons can be made to other animals and plants, respectively, using the sequenced genomes of these two model organisms.

In a paper published in the journal *Nature* in 2003, Dr. Eric D. Green and colleagues reported the comparison of a 1.8 megabase (Mb) region (1,800,000 DNA bases) between 12 different vertebrate organisms. The study showed that humans are more closely related to chimpanzees than to dogs or mice. In this

Figure 9.2 *Arabidopsis,* growing in a culture medium, is a model system for plant genetics research. Plant scientists can use different plants or model systems to study mechanisms of growth and environmental interaction and then apply that knowledge to other plants of agronomic or economic importance.

sequenced region of the human genome lies the gene that, when mutated, causes cystic fibrosis. By locating identical disease-associated regions in other animals like mice and chimpanzees, researchers can use these organisms to glean insight to human gene function under various disease conditions. The benefits of comparative genetics in the above situation are plentiful, including time saving, flexibility, and low cost.

The benefits and possibilities seen with comparative genetics in animals are also attained with plants. *Arabidopsis* is basically a small weed that grows fast, produces a lot of seeds, and

Green Revolution

Dr. Norman Borlaug was a key activist in the rebirth of American agriculture in the middle of the twentieth century. He is credited with initiating the Green Revolution, which was a movement to produce higher yielding crops in response to the population explosion and the reduction in farmland occurring worldwide. High-quality traits of crops from wheat and corn to peas were selected using classical breeding and innovative methods. Plant breeders looked for traits that would make certain plants more productive in grain or fruit. The selected varieties were successful in producing more grain and fruit than the previously cultivated varieties, but there were drawbacks. For one, the more productive plants required large amounts of chemical fertilizer to enhance the size of grain or fruit. Fertilizer is not only expensive, but it can also have toxic methods of production. Therefore, farmers in poor countries had to invest a substantial amount of money in fertilizers. Second, by selecting plants for large fruit traits and removing small fruit plants with other types of genes, the plant breeders inadvertently removed important genes needed for other plant functions, like defense against disease.

In the 1970s, a corn variety called the "Texas male sterile" had been bred for traits ranging from high yield and harvesting ability to disease resistance. Not all of the disease resistant genes, however, had been bred into the Texas male sterile, leaving it vulnerable to previously unimportant pathogens. In fact, one such pathogen, *Helminthosporium maydis*, which causes the southern leaf blight disease, attacked cornfields in the United States, which were 90% Texas male sterile. This disease eliminated half of the corn crops, but luckily some other corn varieties, which had been saved, were quickly planted, reducing the effect of the devastation.

self-fertilizes. *Arabidopsis* is not an agronomically important plant—it isn't grown in fields, harvested, or sold at the grocery store. However, *Arabidopsis* is indirectly agronomically important because information gathered from this plant serves as a model for other plants that are agronomically important. Comparisons have been made between *Arabidopsis* and rice, tomato, corn, and broccoli. *Arabidopsis* homologs, or identical genes, have been found in rice, for example and function similarly in both plants. Michael D. Gale and Katrien M. Devos in 1998 wrote an article titled "Comparative Genetics in the Grasses," published in the scientific journal *Proceedings of the National Academy of Science,* which addressed comparative genetics among nine different grasses. The team of scientists found that many genes and their order on the chromosomes were relatively the same in all nine species. The scientists then concluded that, in the future, grasses with small genomes like rice would be used to study grasses with much larger genomes like corn without having to sequence the entire corn genome. Corn and many plants have genomes that are much larger than that of humans, thus Gale and Devos wrote in their 1998 paper mentioned above, "Comparative genetics will provide the key to unlock the genomic secrets of crop plants with bigger genomes than *Homo sapiens.*"

FUTURE OF PLANT GENETICS

With the advent of automated DNA sequencing technology, whole genomes of microorganisms like bacteria are being sequenced at the rate of two per week! This is an amazing feat if one were to consider that the structure of DNA was discovered only about 50 years ago. Some of the genomes being sequenced in large-scale genomics projects have hundreds of thousands of DNA bases, while others may have hundreds of millions. The amount of information contained within this genetic material must be organized and analyzed through the

Number of Genes in Different Organisms

ORGANISM	GENE NUMBER (approximately)
Arabidopsis	25,000
Humans	25,000
Drosophila (fruit fly)	15,000
Oryza sativa (rice)	50,000
C. elegans (worm)	20,000

Figure 9.3 Genome sizes of a few representative organisms. Given the size of genomes, computer-based programs are required to make genome-wide comparisons.

use of computer-based programs that use math to annotate entire genomes (Figure 9.3).

Whole genome analyses include using genetic resources in conjunction with knowledge of biological processes. As discussed above, genomics can be used to study gene function based on structure and relatedness to genes in other organisms. DNA sequences from genomes are also currently used to predict protein structure and possible protein-protein interactions. The importance of understanding metabolic processes and how they are regulated is a major goal of research projects on organisms across kingdoms. The use of computers and math-based programs to analyze genetic sequences is called bioinformatics. With modern advances in computer technology and even more to come in the future, bioinformatics has emerged as a common and necessary tool for plant and animal geneticists alike.

Glossary

Accession—The identifying number given to a specific variety of plant that is kept in a collection. This number is used to identify the source of genetic material used in research and to order plant material from the collection.

Agrobacterium tumefaciens—A type of microorganism that causes the crown gall disease in some trees. It has been genetically engineered to not cause disease, but rather to insert DNA randomly into the genome of a host plant.

Allele—Form of a gene that can be either dominant or recessive.

Alternation of generations—This process involves the development of both diploid and haploid tissues in the plant. In flowering vascular plants, the most noticeable parts are diploid and the small reproductive cells in the flower are haploid.

Amino acids—The building blocks of proteins, these molecules come together to form peptide chains. There are 20 different types, specified by the triplet codons.

Aneuploids—A general term for a plant or cell that has an abnormal number of chromosomes, either too many or too few, not divisible by the number of chromosomes in the set.

Annotations—Versions of sequence data that are revised using math-based computer programs.

Arabidopsis thaliana—A small, weedy plant in the mustard family, used as a model plant system.

Asexually—Reproduction in which sperm and egg do not mix to form a zygote. The plant can reproduce without fertilization, such as by branching off of an existing root.

Auxin—A plant hormone responsible for normal growth and development, namely vertical growth and root branching.

Avirulence gene—A DNA sequence from a pathogen, coding for a protein that enters the plant host and elicits a response by interacting directly or indirectly with a plant resistance gene (R gene) product.

Bone marrow—The material in the middle of a bone where white blood cells are made and from which adult stem cells can be harvested.

Brassinosteroid—A plant hormone required for normal growth and development.

Breakage-fusion-bridge cycle—Barbara McClintock's term for her discovery that, during meiosis, chromosomes break apart and recombine in different locations while repairing the chromosomes after relocation.

Callus—Undifferentiated tissue; can be induced in the laboratory or by bacteria.

Cell division—The process of creating two cells from one cell, which is the basis for growth of tissues and cell expansion.

Cellulose—The fibrous molecule that makes up the structure of plant cell walls.

Centromere—The point where two chromosome partners connect and are attached to the spindle fibers during meiosis.

Chromatin—Fibrous structure defined by the combination of nucleosomes and chromosomes bound to them. When a genome's DNA is not being replicated or transcribed, it is stored in this form in the nucleus.

Chromosomes—Strand-like structures that are made of DNA and are located in the nucleus of a cell.

Codominance—A non-Mendelian genetic situation in which two equally dominant alleles are expressed and the phenotype is a blending of the two traits.

Codon—A three-letter "word" in which the letters can be any of the four RNA nucleotides: adenine (A), guanine (G), cytosine (C), or uracil (U). The codons refer to specific amino acids and are recognized by transfer RNA molecules.

Colchicine—A chemical found naturally in the autumn crocus plant, used by scientists for doubling the chromosome number in plant cells by preventing separation of chromosome pairs during cell division.

Compatible—An interaction between a plant host and a pathogen in which the plant is not able to elicit a defense response and the plant becomes infected.

Complementation—A test to determine whether a gene candidate is disrupted in a mutant plant by inserting the wild type copy of the gene into the mutant plant.

Glossary

Conserved—Genes that are kept the same and stay in genomes throughout evolution. These are usually vitally important genes.

Cross-fertilization—The process of taking pollen from one plant and using it to pollinate the flower of a different plant.

Crossover event—When the sister chromatids attach at points other than the centromere, leading to exchange of chromosome material; occurs in late prophase I of meiosis.

Cultivars—Subspecies of plants.

Cytogenetics—The study of genetic material using cellular techniques; usually refers to the study of chromosomes.

Cytokinesis—The division of the cytoplasm of a cell, following the last stages in meiosis and mitosis. In plants, this is done by formation of a cell plate.

Cytokinin—A plant hormone responsible for normal growth and development, namely branching of the shoot.

Cytoplasm—The area of a cell that is located between the organelles.

Daughter cells—Cells that have identical genetic material resulting from meiosis.

Dedifferentiate—To become an unspecialized cell or to revert back to a stem cell condition.

Differentiation—The process of becoming a specialized cell.

Diploid—Having two sets of chromosomes in diploid cells and one set in haploid cells. Humans and most animals are diploid, whereas many plants are polyploid.

DNA (deoxyribonucleic acid)—Comprised of any combination of the four nucleotides: adenine (A), guanine (G), cytosine (C), and thymine (T). Provides genetic blueprint for RNA, amino acid, and protein synthesis.

DNA binding protein (DBP)—Protein involved in transcriptional regulation of other genes and signal transduction.

DNA sequence—The combination of the four deoxyribonucleotide bases adenine (A), guanine (G), cytosine (C), and thymine (T).

Dominant—The stronger allele trait.

Dominant negative—A mutant allele that shows a mutant phenotype when in the heterozygous form.

Double fertilization—Unique process in plant reproduction in which one sperm nucleus fertilizes the egg and the other combines with female diploid tissue to make the triploid nutritive tissue called endosperm.

Elicitor—A gene product of a plant pathogen that triggers disease resistance response in incompatible interactions.

Embryo—The earliest form of a new life, having only a few cells, from which all future cells arise.

Embryo sac—The tissue in the female reproductive organ of a plant that becomes a seed after fertilization. Also known as the ovary.

Enhancer—A regulatory region of a gene that activates or increases the expression of a gene when induced.

Enzymatic—Any action involving a protein that leads to completing a function.

Enzyme—A protein that functions to enable a process by catalytic action.

Equilibrium—A balance between two forms.

Ethylene—Plant hormone that causes fruit to ripen.

Euploids—Organisms or cells containing the true number of chromosomes.

Excision—Removal of a piece of DNA (e.g. transposon).

Exon—The DNA sequence of a gene that is transcribed into mRNA and has the information for building the protein product.

Expression—The active transcription of a gene into mRNA, subsequently leading to an end product such as a protein. Scientists look at gene expression to determine whether a gene is functioning.

Fine mapping—A procedure used in forward genetics to precisely locate a gene or DNA sequence on a chromosome.

Forward genetics—An approach to finding genes responsible for a phenotype.

Gametes—Reproductive cells; these cells are the haploid product of meiosis.

Glossary

Gametophytes—The reproductive organs of a plant, found in the flower. For a female flower, this becomes the seed. In a male flower, this is the anther that produces pollen.

Gene—Heritable information in the form of nucleotide sequence (DNA or RNA) that, when expressed, leads to a noticeable trait.

Gene-for-gene resistance—H. H. Flor's model for host-pathogen interaction in plants in which for every pathogen with avirulence gene, there exists a specific plant host resistance gene that recognizes it.

Generations—Genetically similar sets of progeny stemming from the union of gametes hetero- or homogeneously.

Geneticist—A scientist who studies aspects of life science at the gene level.

Genetic material—DNA, RNA, chromosomes, protein, amino acids, and other substances involved in genetic control.

Genetics—The study of heredity and all aspects of inheritable elements.

Genome—The entire nucleotide (DNA or RNA) sequence of an organism.

Genotype—The genetic characterization of a plant or other organism, referring to the alleles found for particular genes, whether homozygous dominant, homozygous recessive, or heterozygous.

Germplasm—Plant materials in the form of seeds, cuttings, or whole plants that can pass on genetic information.

Haploid—Having half the number of chromosomes that are found in somatic cells. In diploid organisms, the haploid number would be just one single set of chromosomes. The cells of this type are also called reproductive cells or gametes.

Heredity—The passing of genetic material from generation to generation.

Heterosis—Extreme hybridization of a plant.

Heterozygous—The state of having one dominant and one recessive allele of the same gene in a given individual.

Hexaploid—Having six sets of chromosomes in the nucleus of somatic cells and three sets in haploid cells. $2n=6x$; $n=3x$.

Homozygous—The state of having two of the same type of allele, either recessive or dominant in a given individual.

Hormones—Class of molecules that are involved in growth and development in physiological processes by being transduced as signals.

Host—A plant that is infected by a pathogen.

Hybrid vigor—The effect of heterosis; mainly strong, robust, high-yielding plants.

Hypothesize—To propose an explanation for a given phenomenon or to pose a question based on scientific data.

Inbreeding depression—The loss of good qualities due to successive and continual self-pollination.

Incompatible—An interaction between a plant host and a pathogen in which the plant is able to elicit a defense response to the pathogen, thereby preventing infection.

Incomplete dominance—A non-Mendelian genetic situation in which both alleles of a gene are expressed and seen in the phenotype without blending traits.

Inheritance—Acquiring genetic material from parents.

Intron—DNA sequence in a gene that is not transcribed to mRNA and therefore does not encode for a part of the protein product.

Inverse-repeat—The short DNA sequences found on the ends of transposons that are exact opposites of each other.

Kinase—An enzyme that has the ability to phosphorylate an amino acid. These enzymes are usually involved in signal transduction pathways that require numerous proteins of this type.

Knock out—A type of mutant in which there is complete disabling of a gene's ability to be expressed.

Late blight—A disease that affects tomatoes and potatoes, caused by a fungus-like microorganism called *Phytopthera infestans*. Responsible for the Irish potato famine of the mid-1800s.

Laws of heredity—Rules of genetic transfer from one generation to the next, based on Mendel's results of garden pea breeding experiments.

Linked—Closely associated, as in two neighboring genes on a chromosome. Genes of this type will not undergo independent segregation.

Glossary

Lycopersicon esculentum—Scientific term for the cultivated tomato.

Mapping—Locating the position of genes on a chromosome.

Mapping population—Collection of plants that are genetically almost identical but vary enough to see phenotypic and genotypic differences. Plants are used to locate markers on the chromosomes, to isolate genes in forward genetics projects.

Markers—DNA sequences used in mapping projects to locate genes by way of counting the number of crossover events between the gene of interest and this sequence.

Megaspore—The haploid female sex cell of a plant. Also known as a megagametophyte.

Megasporocyte—The diploid cell from which the female reproductive cells arise through meiosis.

Meiosis—The process of cell division in which two daughter cells are created from one mother cell, each daughter cell having exactly half the number of chromosomes as the mother cell. This type of cell division creates gametes.

Mendelian—Following the rules of heredity set by Gregor Mendel, based on his garden pea experiments.

Meristem—The area in a plant that holds the stem cells—the shoot apex, the root tip, on floral organs, and along the stem where side branches form.

Messenger RNA (mRNA)—The nucleotide chain that is created in the process of transcription, using a DNA template. The "m" stands for "messenger" because this is the RNA form that translates to transfer RNA and eventually to peptide chains of proteins.

Microorganism—A small life form, such as bacterium, fungus, or yeast whose features can only be seen with the aid of a microscope.

Microspore—The haploid male sex cell of a plant. Also known as the microgametophyte.

Microsporocyte—The diploid cell from which the male reproductive cells arise through meiosis. Also known as the pollen mother cell.

Mitosis—Cell division that results in daughter cells having the same chromosome content as the mother cell.

Mother cell—The originating cell that undergoes meiosis to create two daughter cells.

Mutate—To alter the genetic material in a cell. This may result in a noticeable effect, like in general development or response to environmental factors such as hormones and pathogens.

Mutation—Any change in the genetic material of a cell by any means. For example, addition or deletion of DNA, removal of chromosome pieces, and changing of amino acids in proteins are all ways of changing the genetics of a cell.

Nuclear—Associated with the nucleus of a cell. For example, a nuclear protein that is located or targeted to the nucleus or nuclear pore through which various molecules can pass.

Nucleic acid—The building blocks of DNA and RNA strands comprised of a sugar, a phosphate group, and a ring base.

Nucleosomes—A class of proteins identifiable by their barrel shape, used in holding chromosome threads in chromatin. Chromosome strands are wrapped around the threads of the protein.

Nucleotides—Any of the bases: adenine (A), guanine (G), cytosine (C), thymine (T), or uracil (U) that produce RNA or DNA.

Nucleus—The center of a cell, which contains chromosomes of the entire genome.

Outcross—To cross-fertilize to another plant. Plant breeders may do this to increase heterosis.

Pathogen—A disease-causing parasite.

Pathway—The biochemical chain that is followed in physiological processes.

Peptide—Another name for a protein, which is a chain of amino acids.

Phenotype—Physical characteristics of an organism.

Photomorphogenesis—A change in a plant's position or shape due to varying light conditions.

Photoperiodism—A plant's response to day length.

Physiological—Processes that are involved in maintaining growth.

Glossary

Phytochromes—Red and far-red light-sensing proteins that affect biological processes.

Plasmid—A circular DNA molecule found in bacteria and used in genetic engineering to transform plants.

Pollen—A granular structure of a flower that contains the male sex cell.

Polyploidy—Having more than two sets of chromosomes in somatic cells.

Progeny—Offspring as the result of reproduction.

Promoter—The sequence found before the beginning of a gene on a chromosome that has the ability to either enhance or suppress the gene's expression.

Propagate—To multiply in number by reproduction, either sexually or asexually.

Protease—An enzyme that cuts proteins.

Protein encoding—A gene whose product is a protein as opposed to an RNA structure.

Punnett square—A diagram used to visualize the outcomes of recombination between different alleles of a gene.

Purine—One of the three major parts of nucleic acids, having a double-ring structure. The nucleotides of this form can be either adenine or guanine, depending on the chemical side groups attached to the ring.

Pyrimidine—One of three major parts of nucleic acids, having a single five-sided ring structure. The nucleotides of this form can be either cytosine or thymine (uracil for RNA), depending on the chemical side groups attached to the ring.

Receptors—Proteins or parts of proteins that specifically associate with other molecules, generally leading to a signal transduction.

Recessive—An allele that when in a homozygous state, confers the trait of that allele, but when in a heterozygous state with a dominant allele, masks the trait.

Recombinations—The result of crossover events in which chromosome segments are rearranged in new patterns during meiosis.

Regulatory—Having the ability to alter the course of some function or process by either enabling or inhibiting to various degrees.

Retrotransposon—A transposable element that moves by a copy-and-paste mechanism—first replicating, then inserting the new DNA piece in a new location in the genome.

Reverse genetics—An approach to finding phenotypes due to mutations in known genes.

Reverse transcription—Process of making DNA from an RNA template. Used by some viruses and transposons.

Ribosome—An enzyme that enables replication of DNA into RNA, or vice versa.

RNA (ribonucleic acid)—Comprised of any combination of the four nucleotides: adenine (A), guanine (G), cytosine (C), and uracil (U). Functions to convey genetic information from a DNA template to an amino acid chain. Can also act as a signaling molecule by binding to other nucleic acids or proteins.

RNA polymerase—Enzyme involved in transcription of DNA into RNA by binding to the DNA template strand and synthesizing an RNA copy.

Segregate—To separate, as in the case of dominant and recessive alleles that lead to different traits being expressed in specific ratios.

Self-incompatibility—The rejection (by the stigma) of pollen with the same genotype or from a plant with the same genotype as the stigma on which the pollen lands.

Signaling molecule—Any compound, protein, nucleotide, or atom that can be used to trigger a response when coupled with the appropriate receptor molecule.

Silencer—A regulatory sequence of a gene that, when activated, decreases or inhibits the gene's expression.

S-locus—Gene region containing alleles that are involved in self-incompatibility.

Somatic—The vegetative tissues and organs of plants, such as the root, stem, and leaf.

Glossary

Spindle fibers—Microtubule structures that attach to centers of sister chromatids during meiosis and mitosis, pulling single chromatids to opposite poles.

Sporangia—Part of a plant that is comprised of reproductive cells. The female type has the prefix "mega" and the male has the prefix "micro."

Sporophyte—The diploid generation of a plant.

Stem cell—An undifferentiated cell. In plants, these are found in the meristems.

Stigma—The female part of a flower on which pollen grains land when carried by wind or insects.

Stimuli—Any type of molecule or environmental condition that triggers a response in the plant.

Suppressor—A promoter region that prevents or reduces the transcription of a gene when induced.

Tissue culture—Growth of plants on an artificial nutrient medium.

Totipotency—The unique ability of plant cells to become any type of plant cell, when provided the specific conditions; a stem could become a flower, or a root could become a shoot.

Traits—Physical characteristics, for example the purple color of a flower.

Transcribe—To make mRNA from a DNA template.

Transcription factors (Tfs)—A class of proteins that have the ability to bind to DNA in the nucleus, thereby altering expression of genes. Usually, these proteins are signaled by other proteins from outside the nucleus that transfer the signal through the nuclear envelope where the genes are being transcribed into mRNA.

Transfer DNA (T-DNA)—The segment of a Ti plasmid of *Agrobacterium* that is inserted into the host plant's genome.

Transgenic—Having foreign genetic material in the genome or cell.

Translate—Reading of an mRNA sequence to make proteins.

Transposase—The enzyme responsible for enabling the movement of a transposon.

Transposition—Movement from one location to another, referring to transposons or chromosomal segments that are excised, then reinserted elsewhere in the genome.

Transposon—Piece of DNA containing one or more genes that can move about the genome and insert specifically or randomly, characterized by direct terminal and inverted repeats flanking the sequence.

Triploid—Having three sets of chromosomes in the nucleus of somatic cells and uneven numbers of chromosomes in the haploid cells.

Trisomic—An organism or cell that is normally diploid but has three copies of one of the chromosomes in the set.

True breeding—Plants with a homozygous genotype, so each round of self-fertilization results in offspring with the same genotype as the parent plant.

Ubiquitination—The targeting of proteins for degradation.

Vegetative—Diploid tissue of a plant, referring to the roots, stems, and leaves.

Vegetative reproduction—Asexual process of propagation in which progeny of a plant are exact replicas in genotype of the original plant.

Wild type—Natural or normal form of a gene, as opposed to mutant.

Zea mays—The scientific term for corn.

Zygote—The first cell of a new sexually produced organism. This is formed by the union of sperm and egg, which are each haploid, thus creating a diploid cell.

Bibliography

Bickham, J. W., et al. "Diploid-Triploid Mosaicism: An Unusual Phenomenon in Side-Necked Turtles (*Platemys platycephala*)." *Science* 227 (1985): 1591–1593.

"Biotechnology and the Green Revolution: An Interview with Norman Borlaug." *Actionbioscience.org*. Available online at *http://www.actionbioscience.org/biotech/borlaug.html*.

Brooklyn Botanic Garden. "The Birth of Genetics: Mendel, De Vries, Correns, Tschermak." *Supplement to Genetics* 35, no. 5, pt. 2 (September 1950): 33–47.

Campbell, Neil A. *Biology*. 4th ed. Menlo Park, CA: The Benjamin/Cummings Publishing Company, Inc., 1996.

Corcos, Alain F., and Floyd V. Monaghan. *Gregor Mendel's Experiments on Plant Hybrids*. New Brunswick, NJ: Rutgers University Press, 1993.

Federoff, Nina, and David Botstein, eds. *The Dynamic Genome: Barbara McClintock's Ideas in the Century of Genetics*. Cold Spring Harbor, NY: Cold Spring Harbor Laboratory Press, 1992.

Gallardo, M. H., et al. "Discovery of Tetraploidy in a Mammal." *Nature* 401 (1999): 341.

Gibson, Greg, and Spencer V. Muse. *A Primer of Genome Science*. Sunderland, MA: Sinauer Associates, Inc., 2002.

Hawkes, J. G., N. Maxted, and B. V. Ford-Lloyd. *The* ex situ *Conservation of Plant Genetic Resources*. Boston, MA: Kluwer Academic Publishers, 2000.

Lolle, S. J., et al. "Genome-Wide Non-Mendelian Inheritance of Extra-Genomic Information in *Arabidopsis*." *Nature* 434 (2005): 505–509.

Maxted, N., B. V. Ford-Lloyd, and J. G. Hawkes. *Plant Genetic Conservation: The* in situ *Approach*. London: Chapman and Hall, 1997.

The Multinational *Arabidopsis* Steering Committee. "Progress and Activities of the Multinational *Arabidopsis* Steering Committee (MASC)." *The Multinational Coordinated* Arabidopsis thaliana *Functional Genomics Project: Annual Report 2005* (June 2005): 11–14.

Singh, Ram J. *Plant Cytogenetics*. Boca Raton, FL: CRC Press, 1993.

Snustad, D. Peter, Michael J. Simmons, and John B. Jenkins. *Principles of Genetics*. New York, NY: John Wiley and Sons, Inc., 1997.

Danchin, Antoine. *The Delphic Boat: What Genomes Tell Us.* Cambridge, MA: Harvard University Press, 2002.

Darlington, C. D. *Chromosome Botany and the Origins of Cultivated Plants.* New York, NY: Hafner Press, 1973.

Dash, Joan. *The Triumph of Discovery: Women Who Won the Nobel Prize.* Englewood Cliffs, NJ: Julian Messner, 1990.

Keller, Evelyn Fox. *A Feeling for the Organism: The Life and Work of Barbara McClintock.* San Francisco, CA: W. H. Freeman, 1983.

Somerville, C. R., and E. M. Meyerowitz, eds. *The Arabidopsis Book.* Rockville, MD: American Society of Plant Biologists, 2001. http://www.aspb.org/publications/arabidopsis/.

Websites

The American Institute of Biological Sciences
http://www.actionbioscience.org/

Ag Biosafety
University of Nebraska, Lincoln
http://agbiosafety.unl.edu/

Agricultural Research Service
United States Department of Agriculture
http://www.ars.usda.gov/main/main.htm

American Society of Plant Biologists
http://www.aspb.org/

The Arabidopsis Information Resource (TAIR)
http://www.arabidopsis.org

Council for Biotechnology Information
http://www.whybiotech.com/main.html

DNA from the Beginning,
Cold Spring Harbor Laboratory
http://www.dnaftb.org/dnaftb/

Dolan DNA Learning Center's Gene Almanac
Cold Spring Harbor Laboratory
http://www.dnalc.org/home.html

Further Reading

Mendel Web
http://www.mendelweb.org/

National Biological Information Infrastructure
http://www.nbii.gov/

National Center for Biotechnology Information
http://www.ncbi.nlm.nih.gov/

National Plant Germplasm System, United States Department of Agriculture, Agricultural Research Service
http://www.ars-grin.gov/npgs/

Ucbiotech
University of California
http://ucbiotech.org/

Wayne's Word: An On-line Textbook of Natural History
Palomar College
http://waynesword.palomar.edu/wayne.htm

Index

Index

Index

True breeding
   defined, 4–5
Tschermak, Erich von, 8

Ubquitination, 69

Vavilov, Nicolai Ivanovich, 54
Vegetative state, 38

Vries, Hugo de, 8

Zygote, 49
   chromosomes in, 43, 45
   diploid, 35, 81
   formation of, 5, 33, 42, 80
   unbalanced, 50

page:

6: Peter Lamb
10: Sheila Terry/Photo Researchers, Inc.
12: Gregory G. Dimijian, M.D./
   Photo Researchers, Inc.
14: Joshua T. Williams
19: SPL/Photo Researchers, Inc.
22: Alfred Pasieka/Photo Researchers, Inc.
24: Biophoto Associates/Photo
   Researchers, Inc.
30: Scherer Illustration
31: Scherer Illustration
36: Joshua T. Williams
37: Scherer Illustration
39: Biophoto Associates/Photo
   Researchers, Inc.

46: Astrid & Hanns-Frieder
   Michler/Photo Researchers, Inc.
55: Steve Raymer /CORBIS
57: Bojan Brecelj/CORBIS
67: Joshua T. Williams
68: J. Bavosi/Photo Researchers, Inc.
80: SciMAT/Photo Researchers, Inc.
81: Joshua T. Williams
85: Ted Streshinsky/CORBIS
87: Sally Bensusen/Photo Researchers, Inc.
88: Andrew Syred/Photo Researchers, Inc.
95: Holt Studios/Photo Researchers, Inc.
97: Damien Lovegrove/Photo
   Researchers, Inc.

Cover: Bill Beatty/Visuals Unlimited

About the Author

Carl-Erik Tornqvist is currently a doctoral graduate student studying plant genetics at the University of Wisconsin, Madison. He received his bachelor of science degree from the University of California, Berkeley, in 1999, with a degree in plant biology and genetics. For the three years between receiving his bachelor's and starting graduate school, he was a research associate at the Plant Gene Expression Center in Albany, CA. There he worked with senior scientists on the genetics of disease resistance in the tomato and potato. Born and raised in New Jersey, he became fascinated by plants while helping his father in their home garden. He enjoys traveling, gardening, playing soccer, and cooking lavish meals.

Carl-Erik Tornqvist dedicates this book to his father, Erik Tornqvist, a great scientist who ignited his interest in science. He would also like to acknowledge his family and Jen for their support and critiques. In addition, this book is written in memory of Dr. Anthony B. Bleecker, his former advisor and also a great scientist.